CONTROLLING RESTAURANT & FOOD SERVICE OPERATING COSTS

By Cheryl Lewis & Douglas R. Brown

The Food Service Professionals Guide To:
Controlling Restaurant & Food Service Operating Costs: 365 Secrets Revealed

Atlantic Publishing Group, Inc. Copyright © 2003
1210 SW 23rd Place
Ocala, Florida 34474
800-541-1336
352-622-5836 - Fax

www.atlantic-pub.com - Web site
sales@atlantic-pub.com - E-mail

SAN Number :268-1250

International Standard Book Number: 0-910627-15-0

Library of Congress Cataloging-in-Publication Data

Brown, Douglas Robert, 1960-
Controlling restaurant & food service operating costs : 365 secrets revealed / by Douglas R. Brown & Cheryl Lewis.
p. cm. -- (Food service professionals guide to ; 5)
includes bibliographical references and index.
ISBN 0-910627-15-0 (pbk. : alk. paper)
1. Food service--Cost control. I. Title: Controlling restaurant and food service operating costs. II. Lewis, Cheryl, 1970- III. Title. IV.
Series.
TX911.3.C65 B76 2003
647.95'068'1--dc21
2002013539

Printed in Canada

Book layout and design by Meg Buchner of Megadesign
www.mega-designs.com • e-mail: megadesn@mhtc.net

CONTENTS

Controlling the operating costs of a restaurant is a constant task.

INTRODUCTION

This book deals specifically with ways to reduce operating costs that are primarily management-controllable expenses. Other volumes in this series deal directly with labor, food and beverage costs. Controlling the operating costs of a restaurant is a constant management task. One needs to balance labor, food and liquor costs against sales and quality in order to make any sort of realistic profit. Indeed, it sometimes takes a little lateral thinking to understand that cost savings can be accomplished in a variety of places and in a variety of ways - some of which may be less than obvious!

Thankfully, improvements in technology and management techniques allow smart restaurant operators to keep operating costs within the boundaries needed to generate a profit while still providing their customers with the level of service that they need to generate repeat business. The food service industry is in a state of constant change, particularly due to the nature of pricing fluctuations and rising labor costs. A restaurant manager must be prepared to develop and monitor costs in all controllable areas to maintain profitability.

Some costs you just cannot change. These are the fixed or semi-fixed operating costs, which include such items as union agreements, minimum wage rates, tax rates, rent, permits and fees (such as franchise fees, licensing fees, etc.), insurance and real estate taxes. Fortunately, many costs can be reduced considerably, without reducing quality or efficiency. Some of the controllable and flexible operating costs include purchasing, receiving, storing, food handling, outside services, food preparation, repair and maintenance, advertising, cooking, merchandising, serving methods, staff training, food and beverage cost controls, accounting and legal services, staff productivity, cash handling, housekeeping and sanitation.

As a restaurant operator, you will often find that your bottom line is manipulated by outside circumstances, including competition, weather, quality of your services, food selection, local conventions and events, promotions, discounts, pricing and more. Armed with the information in this book, you will find actual tips that produce profitable results, without consuming all of your time in unnecessary research or, worse, experiences of painful trial, risk and error. This book also lists company names and contact information with corresponding tips, where appropriate.

CHAPTER ONE

THE BOTTOM LINE

Basic Cost-Control Skills

The first skill you need when running a restaurant does not involve whipping up a hollandaise sauce or steaming broccoli. The first skill you need is to have a grip on accounting and cost-control. When you understand the financial side of the food service business, you can then make small tweaks on an almost-daily basis to increase your bottom line. Neglect to pay attention to the numbers and you may not even realize how much money you are losing. Presently, throughout the entire food service industry, operating expenses are up and income is down. After taxes and expenses, restaurants that make money, according to the National Restaurant Association, have net bottom lines at 0.5-4 percent of sales. This tiny percentage is the difference between being profitable and going under. This drives home the importance of controlling your costs and understanding the numbers. A lot can be done to control costs and it begins with planning. The decision to succeed in the food service industry will require serious planning, structured thought and hard work. So, where do you start? Here are a few essential basics:

- **Get computerized.** No matter what type or size of your food service operation, our advice is get your operation computerized, at least the back office operations. It's extremely difficult to compete successfully without utilizing technology, at least to some degree. Today the investment for a basic computer and accounting software is less than $2,000 and could be as little as $1,000. The investment will deliver immediate insight into your business and savings in accounting fees.

- **QuickBooks®.** Our favorite general restaurant accounting package, based upon cost and features, is the veteran QuickBooks® by Intuit. The QuickBooks® 2002 version is rich in features, including built-in remote-access capabilities and Web interfaces. Reports are generated in a few seconds that would take hours to calculate manually. The reports are also flawless, eliminating the human-error factor. This program now has a POS option that was the only limiting factor prior to this new release. QuickBooks® is available at www.quickbooks.com. Another popular accounting package is Peachtree®, available at www.peachtree.com.

- **Tasty Profits software.** If you're just setting up your accounting program and decide to use QuickBooks®, we recommend an add-on product called "The Tasty Profits Guide to QuickBooks® Software for Restaurants." This helpful guide to QuickBooks® enables you to save thousands of dollars doing your own accounting with its proven, easy-to-use system. Simply install the floppy disc that is included with the "Tasty Profits Guide" directly into your computer. Download the pre-configured restaurant accounts and you're ready to go. You will have instant access to all your financial data; be able to calculate accurate food, labor and liquor costs with ease; reconcile bank and credit card statements; track and pay tips that are charged to credit cards; and calculate sales tax automatically. The program costs about $70 and is available at www.atlantic-pub.com, 800-541-1336 (Item TP-01).

Establishing Controls - Financial, Budgeting and Organizational

Establish your control systems by using the following straightforward steps:

- **Overview.** Define your business goals and objectives.
- **Business plan.** If you haven't already done so, develop a business plan that spells out, in detail, how your goals and objectives are to be achieved.
- **Organizational plan.** Develop an organizational structure that can achieve the desired objectives and goals.
- **Put it in writing.** Set up policies and procedures to be followed by the staff.
- **Hire and train management and operating personnel**.
- **Implement the plan.** Make regular corrections and adjustments to meet goals.
- **Operational controls.** Important! A restaurant needs to exercise control in a number of operating areas. Budgetary control is used to help achieve these objectives. The main operational areas include:
    - The quality of food and beverages
    - Employee costs and performance
    - The control of equipment, utilities and other physical assets
    - Control over sales and cash
    - Operating expenses

Developing a Food Service Operational Budget - The Basics

Put financial control implements into action by first making a budget. QuickBooks® and other software programs can assist you with this. The great advantage of using one of these software programs is you can easily compare your budget to your actual figures any time you like in a matter of seconds. Here are the basics:

- **Gather the essential information.** Management needs to collect the following types of information:
  - Actual operating statements and budget figures from the previous year
  - The restaurant's financial goals
  - Sales statistics broken down for each category from the past
  - Any change in restaurant operating policies, e.g., eliminating lunch service or adding a catering service
  - Regional, local and national economic conditions
  - Sales and expense trends in all categories
  - Menu prices, customer preference, portion size and food costs
  - Payroll information

Follow these basic steps to prepare a budget:

- **Estimate sales revenue.** This is often the most difficult part of the budget due to its volatility.

- **Estimate expenses** that are related to sales such as food, liquor, wine and operational supplies.

- **Use industry resources and your sales history to help you come up with an operating budget.** You can find restaurant business information and publications that give guidance with setting up budgets at the National Restaurant Association's Web site at www.restaurant.org.

Key Operating Budget Costs

Your operating budget will reflect your priorities in terms of how you spend your money, the expenses you will incur and how you will meet those expenses (income).

If you're a start-up operation, your operating budget should also include money to cover the first 3-6 months of operation. It should allow for the following expenses:

- Personnel
- Food costs
- Liquor costs
- Operating expenses
- Insurance
- Rent
- Depreciation
- Loan payments
- Advertising/promotions
- Legal/accounting
- Supplies
- Payroll expenses
- Salaries/wages
- Utilities
- Dues/subscriptions/fees
- Taxes
- Repairs/maintenance
- Miscellaneous expenses

Sales Reports and Forecasting

A simple tool to assist you in the budgeting process is a Sales History Form. Financial statements are great, but this will help you remember specifics from a year ago. Use sales and expense forecasting and market research to track how many customers you are currently serving, what they eat and how often they visit your restaurant. Compare this information with how many customers you want to be serving, what they want to eat and how often they might return. The following guidelines will help:

- **Sales history.** Basically, a sales history tells you what you have done in sales in the past and helps you forecast what to expect in the future. This form should record customer counts, daily sales and daily costs.

- **Here's a simplified example of a sales history.** Remember, the more information you track, the more information you have at your disposal to help with cost-cutting decision making:

Date	Lasagna # / $	Ravioli # / $	Daily Sales	Daily Costs	# Customers
3-15	14/$149.95	22/$220.90	$1,249.50	$562.90	97
NOTES: Training a new cook – Jim Provolone, severe snow storm predicted tonight					

- **Use your sales history.** In the above example, the manager can compare this date with the same date last year. By looking at the note column in the sales history, the manager can see that on this particular date, the restaurant may have been running a higher cost because of the training. Sales will be down due to the weather.

- **POS.** Computerized registers known as point-of-sale systems, or POS, can do most of this work for you. For a comparison of many of the electronic systems available, log on to www.cookeryonline.com/Link%20Frames/POS.html. The Web site www.semicron.com/rpe2001.html also offers a point-of-sale system.

- **Study your monthly profit and loss statements.** This statement, also known as a P & L statement, will include the following information: net sales, cost of sales, operating expenses, operating profit, taxes on income and net income. An income statement displays the profit or loss that a company has realized over a specific period, such as a year. The statement reports sales, cost of sales and all the other expenses. The margin between sales and costs equals the profit or loss. Your P & L statement tells far more than you may realize if it is in the proper industry format.

- **The Uniform System of Accounts for Restaurants.** The National Restaurant Association publishes a simple, easy-to-use accounting classification system for restaurants. This valuable book, prepared by CPAs, includes examples of balance sheets, wage-control reports and an expense-classification system. If you take only one idea from this book, we recommend you use this system. You can order online at www.restaurant.org, or by calling 800-424-5156. The Uniform System of Accounts for Restaurants (USAR) is an essential guide for restaurant accounting. It establishes a common industry language that allows you to compare ratios and percentages across industry lines. The goal of this comparison is to create financial statements that are management tools, not just IRS reports. Industry accounting representatives have designed the system and have incorporated their collective restaurant experience into the system. If you are using QuickBooks® and the add-on software Tasty Profits®, your information will be in this format. Since the system is uniform, comparisons can be made between different restaurants and/or different time periods in your restaurant. The National Restaurant Association collects accounting information from numerous restaurant companies and publishes the consolidated numbers in industry statistical reports. By comparing your establishment's percentages to other restaurant operations, you can pinpoint possible cost-control problem areas.

- **Operations report.** The National Restaurant Association also publishes a report, "The Operations Report," based on an annual survey of operator income statements. Conducted jointly by the association and the accounting firm of Deloitte & Touche, the report provides detailed data on where the restaurant dollar comes from and where it goes for four categories of restaurants: three types of full-service operations (with per-person check sizes under $10; between $10 and $25; and $25 and more) and limited-service operations (fast food).

- **Utilize the same chart of accounts to compare your operation with others.** Ratios enable you to compare the operating data of a specific restaurant to the average for a group of similar establishments. You may, for example, compare the assets of a particular restaurant with the average assets of restaurants of a similar size in order to determine if it is as financially healthy as it should be. You can easily compare operating costs and other costs for comparisons.

Cash Flow - The Essentials

Consultants who specialize in restaurant businesses say that owners/managers don't pay enough attention to cash flow, which, in simple terms, is the measure of how much money you really have in the business. You'll need to get to grips with the following basics:

- **Statement of cash flows.** This most important report tells you if your business is on or off target. Use your own computer program to generate this report or get your accountant to run a report NOW! A statement of cash flows starts with the bottom of your profit and loss statement - the line that shows your net income. Several adjustments are then made to that number, including reducing the income by invoices recorded as income that have not yet been paid, adding back depreciation, adjusting for bills that your business has not paid and several other adjustments.

- **Funds.** Your organization can accomplish very little without adequate funds. Ensure your cash reserves are adequate to cover slow months, make emergency repairs and improvements and implement marketing projects.

- **Set realistic targets and goals for growth for your business.** For example, aim to acquire 100 new repeat customers every month. Lower operating expenses next month by 2 percent. By letting your staff know that they can do their part, you will be able to meet your goals and build your business accordingly.

Renting and Leasing

The following tips can make a big difference in reducing your restaurant operating costs.

- **Plan early for lease re-negotiations.** At least a year before your lease expires, evaluate and analyze other rental options and costs. This will leave you about six months to negotiate with the owner.

- **Consider taking on a longer lease.** Request a break in the monthly lease payments and ask for an annual inflator clause in return for signing a longer lease. Also request a few more months of free rent than you need when renewing your lease since this is often the easiest negotiating point for landlords to offer as an incentive.

- **Place caps on escalator clauses.** Make sure that your rent doesn't rise dramatically if inflation increases. Since operating-expense clauses are broadly defined, they tend to favor the landlord.

- **Place a maximum cap on your share of yearly operating costs increases.** This is called common area management (CAM) in shopping centers. If your share of operating costs seems excessive, use a "lease auditor" to analyze the terms. They should determine if all the operating costs being charged back to you are allowable under terms of the lease. Check the Yellow Pages to locate a lease auditor in your city. Try to get options to renew your lease and lock in low rates for several years.

- **Space.** Verify the accuracy of the "square footage" specified as the "rentable space" upon which your payments are calculated. Measure your space carefully and compare it with the square footage stated in your lease.

- **Try using a third party** to do the preliminary negotiations.

- **Research the lease terms of other tenants in the building.** Find out what concessions they are receiving and about their plans for moving.

- **Question the Common Area Management.** Compare your CAM charges with national averages that are available from the Urban Land Institute at 1025 Thomas Jefferson St. NW, Suite 500 West, Washington, D.C. 20007, 800-321-5011; www.uli.org or www.icsc.org. Insert an amendment giving you the right to include audit costs in the CAM. Look for clauses that say "CAM charges include but aren't limited to." Detail CAM expenses that are excluded such as structural repairs or depreciation.

- **Watch for commonly used landlord clauses.** Examples include:
  - Requiring a tenant to pay for unlimited future increases in operating expenses.
  - Obligating you to pay for costs of other tenants who ring up high utilities charges.
  - Allowing eviction if you do not maintain a high enough sales volume.

- Making you comply with new mall operating hours that would be unprofitable .
- Requiring you to pay for capital expenditures that may be referred to as "reserves and replacements."

- **Analyze the details in your lease billing.** Pinpoint miscalculations, wrong rates, inaccurate square footage and overcharges for pass through and items not authorized by the lease contract. Lease analysis experts estimate approximately 30 percent of commercial lease arrangements result in over billing.

- **Request the ability to sublease your space.**

Insurance Costs

All of your insurance products should be reviewed every year. Take a closer look at the following issues:

- **Liability insurance.** If you have liability insurance, you may need a higher amount of coverage. You may want to adjust your deductibles based on past experience and you may be due a better rate because of your claim history.

- **Compensation.** With workers' compensation insurance, you need to make sure that your employees are properly classified. Consider removing the owner from workers' compensation if covered elsewhere.

- **Premiums.** Your premium is based on a rate assigned to each classification of employee and the amount of gross wages paid. Certain job descriptions put an employee at greater risk than others, such as a chef versus an office bookkeeper.

- **Health insurance.** You also should review your health insurance coverage and shop the market for group programs that may be more suited to your employee base. Look closely at the invoices you receive from your health insurance carrier; you will be amazed at what you may find - employees who have not worked for you in months, family premiums for single individuals, etc. Put someone in charge of reviewing this invoice every month to ensure that you are paying the correct amount for eligible employees only.

Equations for Your Business

Figuring your costs, income or expenses is fairly simple once you know the formulas for doing so. Simply use these basic formulas to decipher these simple business issues:

- **Calculating the controllable operating-, food-- and beverage-cost percentages.** Take your cost of all food sold, divide by the food revenue and then multiply by 100 to find your food cost percentage:

  (Total Food Cost ÷ Total Food Revenue) x 100 = Actual Food-Cost Percentage

  For example, your total monthly food cost is 40,000. Your total food sales for that same year is $100,000.

  (40,000÷100,000) x 100 = 40%

- **Calculating target food costs.** In order to make this figure useful to you in finding ways to cut expenses, you'll also need to determine your target food cost. Let's say your target food cost is 35 percent. Now, what actions can you take to decrease your actual food cost? We'll talk about this in more detail in the next chapter.

- **Number of guests required to be served to break even.** Take your average of the guest checks, subtract the variable costs per guest and then divide that into the total fixed costs to find the number of guests.

- **Number of guests required to be served to meet rising variable costs.** Add your old variable costs and the additional variable costs that you now have, take that number and subtract it from the guest check average and write that number down (this will be B). Next, take the total fixed costs and add the desired net income you require (A). Then, take "A" and divide by "B" to find how many more guests you will need to serve to meet your expenses.

- **Number of guests required to serve to meet income goals.** Take the total fixed costs and add your desired income (A), then use your customer check average less the variable cost per guest (B). "A" divided by "B" will give you how many customers you must serve in order to meet your income goals.

- **Finding your guest check average.** The total annual revenues divided by the total number of guests gives you this average.

- **Figuring the labor needed per guest.** Take your total labor costs for a period of time, divide by the number of guests for the set period of time and the answer will be how much labor is involved.

- **Calculating the yield percentage involved in your recipe.** Take the product loss divided by the weight required for portioning.

Getting Organized

Organization is the greatest, cheapest manner available to generate productivity and reduce costs. The mere act of putting instructions on paper, or giving your staff a checklist instead of having to hold their hand through a process, can save your company thousands in labor, preventative maintenance and productivity. Try the following approach:

- **Organizational and structural component charts.** Use organizational charts to know exactly who does what in your restaurant on a daily, weekly and monthly basis. How can this structure improve? Are jobs allocated in the most productive manner possible? Written job descriptions are good tools to use for this. You can find examples of job descriptions and a questionnaire for writing job descriptions at www.hrnext.com. Atlantic Publishing offers a complete set of job descriptions on computer disk at www.atlantic-pub.com.

- **Standardized procedures.** Do you provide your staff with standardized recipe cards, bar recipes, opening procedures, closing procedures and instructions as to how you want each process followed? If it's not on paper, it's far easier to ignore or vary the ways things should be done.

- **Job lists.** Create a list of tasks specific for each position. Post them in a prominent position. For your servers and cooks, for example, make a list for opening and closing responsibilities. You should also post tasks that should be done during slow periods, such as cleaning out the walk-in or refilling salt and pepper shakers. By making these lists readily available, you will encourage employees to complete these tasks in a timely fashion rather than search for a manager to ask what they should do or assume they don't need to do anything during slow times.

- **Use checklists.** Create a checklist of items you perform every day. Organize your time. Of course, variations from this checklist will always occur, but you'll cover the basics a lot faster with a guide in hand. It saves you and your staff time and avoids confusion.

- **Are you writing and rewriting lists?** Get organized by having a large quantity of forms made to meet your checklist needs. Use bulletin boards throughout your establishment to communicate information to your staff. These can be used to post job duties, daily specials, new policies, schedules, etc.

- **How many magazines/newspapers/industry journals can you read each month?** If you have a reading pile on your desk, consider scaling down on the reading material subscriptions. Not only will you save money, but you'll also give yourself more time to make sense of what you read.

- **Fees and penalties.** Extra fees, penalties and late charges can really stack up and hurt a business, but a little common sense and planning can limit or eliminate these charges, allowing you to stay on budget and steer clear of avoidable costs.

- **Credit accounts.** Do you allow regular customers to run credit accounts? Keep your collection expenses to a minimum by only allowing the largest of businesses and most reliable of customers to run an ongoing tab. This will radically cut down your collection expenses and uncollectible debts.

- **Don't delay tax payments.** Paying your sales and usage taxes when they are due allows you to avoid costly penalties and tax interest fees, which results in large savings to your bottom line. Similarly, many communities and states offer discounts for paying your property and sales taxes early.

- **Help on staff tips from the IRS.** There is a tax credit available to all restaurants with tipped employees. The credit amount is added to profits then subtracted from income taxes owed. The credit represents the FICA paid on tips used to bring earnings up to minimum wage. Check with your accountant as this area is tricky and constantly changing.

- **Debt.** If at all possible, pay off all business debt. Debt is one of the major causes of failure among small businesses today. Interest on loans can quickly eat away at your profits.

- **Are you utilizing all the discounts available to you?** Many bills offer discounts for advance or prompt payment, especially when it comes to utility bills. Also, your suppliers will often run specials on end-of-line items, slow movers, new products or things that they've managed to acquire at a better-than-normal rate.

Try to look at your restaurant the way others see it.

CHAPTER TWO

TAKE AN OBJECTIVE LOOK AT YOUR RESTAURANT

An Overview

It's often easy, when you get distracted by day-to-day tasks, to fail to see your establishment in the same way as others see it. There could be a lot going on that you wouldn't agree with right under your nose, but how do you step back and get an outsider's perspective? Here are some suggestions:

- **Check the competition.** Dine in your competitors' establishments - often. Note where they have you beat and where you're outdoing them. Take notice of any other owners eating in your restaurant while you're there and try to figure out what ideas they might be taking away, or what deficiencies they may be spotting. Dining at your competition will save you expenses in terms of experimentation. For example, if their lunchtime special isn't bringing in the customers, maybe you should abandon any plans to match them. It will also help you figure out which of your strengths to concentrate on and weaknesses on which to work.

- **Online information about the competition.** A good resource to check on the competition is at www.restaurantnews.com/financials.html. This page gives you financial information for over 50 restaurant chains throughout the United States!

- **Customer surveys.** Use customer surveys to find out what your customers want from your restaurant, what makes them happy and what they don't like. Try to meet their demands. Have your servers give customers the survey and a pen with their check and allow them time to sit after their meal so they can fill out the form. You may want to consider giving your customers a thank-you token, such as a coupon for a free appetizer for their help. Surveying customers will not only tell you how to make your patrons happier, it may also uncover ways to cut costs. For example, your survey results show that the majority of your customers don't eat the packaged crackers you serve with salads. You may want to consider getting rid of these crackers (and their expense) or replacing them with a cheaper alternative.

- **Hire a mystery shopper to go undercover and check out your business.** A mystery shopper plays the role of a "regular customer." They compile the information on their customer experience into a report to you. They'll tell you how helpful the servers were, how well the food was presented, how it tasted, how clean the restaurant was, how long they had to wait for their table and meal and what improvements need to be made. Find them online at www.secretshopnet.com (Secret Shopper), www.mysteryshopperjobs.com (Mystery Shopper) and www.mysteryshop.com (Mystery Shop).

- **Consider being the mystery shopper yourself.** Or, send a couple of employees to do research. The cost would only be that of a meal!

Surveys

Surveys and market research are a great way to find out what's really going on in the minds of customers, potential customers and employees. Try the following:

- **Web sites.** For ideas on how to create surveys for your customers, locals and staff, visit these Web sites:
    - profiler.hprtec.org/survey_creation
    - www.custominsight.com
    - www.surveysite.com
    - www.formsite.com
    - www.hostedsurvey.com

- **Survey cards.** Monitor customers to find out which advertising they remember. Hand out survey cards for each customer, asking them where they heard or read about your establishment.

Market Research

Market research is an important way to find out what type of customer you should be targeting, what these customers spend on eating out and what they want. Here are some Web sites that offer market research information:

- **MarketReasearch.com.** This Web site has market research for the restaurant industry available for downloading. Costs run anywhere from $200 to several thousand dollars for reports that include titles such as Fast Food in the USA; Dining Out Market Review; and Top Market Share Sandwich, Pizza and Chicken Chain Restaurants Survey.

- **American FactFinder**. This Web site, factfinder.census.gov/servlet/BasicFactsServlet, lets you search, browse and map U.S. Census' data, including economic, population, geographical and housing statistics.

- **CACI Information Decision Systems.** This site allows you to order demographic information by zip code. Pricing is by subscription or information can be priced per requested report. Log on to www.infods.com for a free sample of reports and a free zip code search.

- **Service Annual Survey.** This part of the U.S. Census' Web site offers annual estimates of receipts for some service industries. This information can be found at www.census.gov/svsd/www/sas.html.

- **U.S. Bureau of Economic Analysis.** This Department of Commerce agency hosts a Web site at www.bea.gov, which provides publications and data on businesses by industry.

CHAPTER THREE

TRIMMING OPERATIONAL COSTS

Office Expenses

As much as you'd like to avoid office, electricity, gas, phone, food, labor and beverage expenses, they're a fact of life. But you don't have to let these expenses run out of control. With a few simple rules and an eye on the bottom line, you can keep those expenses down to a minimum. Here's how:

- **Use part-time employees.** You may find that part-time personnel with a confirmed list of duties will be less inclined to "fill time." Additionally, depending on the length of the shift, a part-time employee might not need a meal break, which is another expense. You also can save money on benefits, such as health insurance, retirement plans, etc., by using part-time employees.

- **Outsourcing.** If some office tasks are too important to leave in the hands of inexperienced, busy or part-time employees, consider outsourcing the task to an expert in the field. Outsourcing your bookkeeping to a professional who comes in one day a week is far more cost effective. To compare rates for human resources outsourcing services, log on to www.BuyerZone.com.

- **Compare prices online.** Comparison-shopping sites compare prices from a number of online shops. Comparison sites cover virtually everything available for purchase. Try www.google.com, dmoz.org or www.crosssearch.com

- **Buy printing online.** You can secure bids from and deal directly with a range of domestic and international printing companies by posting your job specs on the Printing Industry Exchange™ Web site of www.printindustry.com. Printers will then send their bids straight to you - and you'll deal directly with them throughout the job. On the other hand, why use a printing company at all when you can create your own office stationery? With a PC or Mac, some nice card stock, a laser printer and some graphic software (such as Quark and/or Photoshop), it is possible to create your own business cards, flyers and menus without going out-of-house. If you have the time and talent, get to it!

- **Menu design and printing software.** Quality menu printing can cost you a lot of money, so do yourself a favor and laminate your menus so that they're waterproof and easy to clean. With the advent of the personal computer, there have been a few menu design software programs developed in recent years. The software is generally very easy to use, with built in templates, art work, etc. Your finalized menu can be printed out on a laser printer. Color, clip art, photos, art work and graphics may be added. One such software program is Menu Pro™. An extensive demonstration of the software may be found at www.atlantic-pub.com, or call 800-541-1336.

- **Payroll.** Try QuickBooks®. Get a quote from online payroll service firms to see if outsourcing this task will save you money. If payroll recordkeeping is a significant part of a full-time bookkeeper's time, then outsourcing it may enable you to realize savings by going to part-time help. Outsourcing may also be a solution to problems with costly payroll accounting staff turnover and training costs. Online payroll Web sites include: Payroll Online, EasyPayNet, PayMaxx, Paychex and Oracle Small Business Suites Payroll.

- **To save time on mailing and paperwork, consider using an electronic bill-paying service.** It works especially well for recurring monthly bills. By timing your bill payments electronically, you can wait until the last due date and stretch your working capital. QuickBooks® has an electronic bill-paying service built into the program. Companies like CheckFree license their bill payment engine to financial institutions, so ask your bank if they offer this service at a reasonable cost. Before signing up for this service, compare the cost of paying your bills online with your current process. Web sites that connect you to the convenience of electronic bill payment include: eBillPay (free for 6-month trial), Oracle Small Business Suite, Checkfree.com, StatusFactory, Yahoo BillPay, Paytrust.com and PayMyBills.com.

- **Consider bulk mail.** If you advertise by sending out circulars, you should look into using bulk mail rates. Log on to the United States Post Office Web site at www.usps.com/directmail for more information on using bulk and direct mail for marketing.

- **Is postage use monitored in your office?** Is postage only used for business needs or do employees sometimes throw their phone bill check in with your invoice payments? Who has access to the postage meter or postage stamps?

- **Watch for telephone solicitations.** Be skeptical of unsolicited calls, particularly for office supplies and toner for office machines. These scammers will often act as if they know you and then ask for the model of your printer of copy machine. They will then ship and bill you for replacement parts, toner, etc., that you didn't order. Designate certain employees as buyers with authority to issue purchase orders for supplies. Then check documentation, such as purchase orders, before paying bills or accepting shipments. If the vendor ships items that are different from the brand, quantity, or quality you ordered, you can legally treat it as unordered merchandise. To find information about common scams and report fraud, go to the Federal Trade Commission's Web site on office supply scams at www.ftc.gov.

- **Use postcards.** Use creative, attention-grabbing postcards instead of always producing a more elaborate, costly mailing piece. Since they are not heavily used for direct mailing, individual postcards stand out. With large savings in postage, production and lead times, postcards can be a cost-effective way to build traffic with a captivating photo or illustration on one side and compelling copy on the other. Even plain postcards with a personal note to customers or prospects can get powerful results for about 30 cents.

Trim Phone Expenses

Many business operators don't even look at their utility bills, but those that do can often find ways to reduce their monthly outlays on phone calls with a little smart thinking and forward planning. Consider the following:

- **Do you know who is using your business telephone** and where they are calling?

- **How long do your employees spend on the phone?** Do they use it while on a break, at lunch, before work, after work or during time that they should be spending on customers? Make it a blanket rule that employees should not have access to restaurant phones unless they are engaging in specifically outlined business activities (such as taking orders and reservation calls).

- **Make a pay phone available in the restaurant for your employees' needs.** This will not only save you money, but can actually make you money as most pay phone operators work on a profit-share basis with the establishment they're in. Visit G-Tel at www.payphone.com, 800-884-4835.

- **Keep an employee phone log.** If employees must use your office phone, consider keeping a log of all employee phone use and to where the call was made so that any toll charges can be paid by the employee, not your business.

- **Do you need unlimited calling set up for your fax line?** If your fax always seems to be in use, this may save you additional fees and taxes.

- **Flexibility.** You may want to consider having a cell phone or cordless telephone handy so you can address business calls while you're moving about your establishment. If you don't have a cordless telephone, you will find yourself constantly being called back into the office to answer the phone. Not only will it cost you time in your daily activities, but also money!

- **Cut the cord.** Get free cellular phones equipped with nationwide calling. Use the cell phones for all long-distance calls.

- **Use "800" numbers.** When calling a vendor, don't use their direct number if it will be a long-distance call. Instead, use their "800" number.

- **Compare long-distance rates and carriers available in your area** at least once every three months. Are you getting the best deal? Consider changing your telephone carrier if you can get a better deal and always ask for a rate better than advertised. You'll be surprised how often you can get what you ask for!

- **Long distance.** To compare long-distance phone rates between multiple suppliers, try using the following sites: Lower My Bills at www.lowermybills.com or Telecommunication Research at www.trac.org.

- **Check your phone contracts and bills.** Ensure that you are on the right tax and are paying for the right tax. Also, check that you are receiving the appropriate discounts and that all phone lines are covered by the discounts.

- **Fax it.** Faxing is less expensive than mailing and using a computer/fax modem is the least expensive and saves the most time, paper and ink. One analysis shows that labor cost per page will run about 15 cents for mailing compared with 2 cents for faxing.

- **Fax lines.** Do you have too many phone lines? Can some be cancelled? Consider eliminating your dial-up account line and a fax line by switching to a cable modem or DSL and then using e-mail as a fax such as E-Fax, www.e-fax.com, or max-e-mail, www.maxemail.com.

- **Use a low-tariff telecoms provider for long-distance or international calls.** Use selective call blocking (say, on international calls) and call log recording to highlight any misuse.

Energy Expenses

According to the National Restaurant Association, an average restaurant spends 2 percent of its revenue on energy and only 0.05-4 percent of its gross revenue becomes profit. So, if a restaurant owner reduces energy consumption by 25 percent, profit will increase from 4 to 4.5 percent of revenue, the same as a 12.5 percent increase in sales. Even the smallest cost-saving procedure can save you thousands of dollars a year if you stick with it. EPA research breaks down energy use by a typical restaurant as follows: cooking (23 percent), water and space heating (19 percent each), lighting (11 percent), cooling (8 percent), refrigeration (6 percent), ventilation (5 percent) and office equipment (1 percent) to name the big ones. Tightening just one practice can lead to long-term savings. Consider the following possibilities:

- **Most electric companies have departments devoted to helping you reduce power costs.** Call your local electricity supplier and ask them to send someone out to help you keep costs and wastage to a minimum and they'll, in all likelihood, do so for free.

- **Use timers on everything.** Use timers for all of

your lights in case employees forget to shut them off at the end of the day. The use of timers will ultimately create savings in your electrical costs and can also be used as a break-in deterrent to give the impression someone is in the building late at night. In addition, install timers to turn water heaters off when the restaurant is closing and to turn them on two hours before opening in order to reach the desired temperature. Consider installing a solar water heating device.

- **Often employees will carelessly leave a light on in walk-in coolers.** Consider using a timer or motion detector on these lights so that a few minutes after an employee forgets to shut off the lights, they automatically turn off. Also be sure that employees shut walk-in and reach-in doors completely. This can be a huge energy drain!

- **Air-conditioning.** Many air-conditioning systems are designed to work at a low rate, even when the temperature is perfect, just to keep air flow moving. If you have windows and doors that can be opened during a nice breezy day, have the A/C turned off altogether.

- **Consider adding a heat pipe system.** This can dramatically improve the moisture removal capabilities of many air-conditioning systems, yet actually lower power bills at the same time. Air can be pre-cooled by simply transferring heat from the warm incoming air to the cool supply air. This "bypassing" can be accomplished by placing the low end of a heat pipe in the return air and the high end in the supply air. Heat is removed from the warm upstream air and rerouted to the cool downstream air. This heat, in effect, bypasses the evaporator - although the air that contained the heat does indeed pass through the A/C coil. The total amount of cooling required is slightly reduced and some of the air conditioner's sensible capacity is therefore exchanged for additional latent capacity. Now the unit can cope with high-moisture air more efficiently. See www.heatpipe.com/heatpipes.htm or www.lanl.gov/orgs/pa/science21/HeatPipes.html for more information.

- **Cleanliness and efficiency.** The coils on the back of your refrigerators and coolers work far less effectively when they're clogged with dust, ice and grease. Ensure that at least every two months, a staff member turns off the refrigerators for 10 minutes and cleans the coils thoroughly. Also, drain and flush hot water heaters every 6 months to remove minerals that have settled on the bottom of the tank.

- **Look into a switching service.** In many areas, gas and electric companies have become deregulated. If your business is in one of these areas, do some research to see if your current carrier is giving you the best possible rates.

- **Use lower-wattage light bulbs.** Look for longer-lasting light bulbs that don't require as much energy. Halogen lights are another good alternative. They're more expense to purchase, but they last a good deal longer than fluorescent lights. Retrofit with energy-efficient lighting. Specifically, re-lamp to lower-wattage bulbs. Switch from incandescent to high-efficiency fluorescent. Install dimmers, motion sensors and photocells to control lighting automatically. Dimmable ballasts are available for T-8s as well as a new generation of compact fluorescents. Consider high-pressure sodium or low-wattage metal halide lamps for outdoor lighting. Install compact fluorescents in the kitchen exhaust hoods. Replace all light bulbs with energy-efficient fluorescent bulbs. According to the EPA's Energy Star Small Business advisors, converting fluorescent fixtures to T-8 fluorescent bulbs with electronic ballasts can save 20-50 percent a year.

- **Have a contractor look at your property to calculate your building's heat loss.** All buildings lose heat through windows, doors, the roof, etc. Have someone look at your building to pinpoint areas that may need your attention. Perhaps your windows need weather-stripping, or you may need to add additional insulation in spots.

- **Turn off equipment.** Turn off personal computers and copiers at night if not in use. If left running all night long, one office's PC may waste more power than the lights used all day. Also, turn kitchen appliances off when not in use. Remember, most kitchen equipment takes less than 20 minutes to pre-heat.

Extra Energy-Saving Tips

Here are some more tips for making big savings on energy costs:

- **Implement an equipment startup/shutdown schedule.** Draw up a step-by-step startup/shutdown checklist. Ask all employees to follow this routine.

- **Mirrors.** The use of mirrors throughout your

establishment will maximize the effect of your lighting as well as give your room the illusion of increased space.

- **Turn exhaust hoods off** when the appliances are not in use.

- **Infrared fryers.** Replacing a conventional gas fryer with an infrared gas fryer can boost profits by as much as $600 a year.

- **Turn parking lot lighting off** automatically with a photocell.

- **Walk-in freezers or coolers.** Installing a plastic strip curtain over the entrance can save up to $200 a year per refrigerator. See www.traxindprod.com, www.rackandshelf.com or www.koroklear.com.

- **Coffee warming.** Bunn-O-Matic, www.bunnomatic.com, has designed special lids for its coffee makers to keep steam and heat from leaving the coffee - a move that not only saves coffee-warming energy, but also the extra energy required to condition the air. Always store coffee in insulated containers instead of on the holding coils of the machine. This will ensure quality and reduce energy loss.

- **Make sure you replace furnace filters on a regular basis.** Clogged filters can cause a furnace to overheat and shut down.

- **Sensors.** Install sensors or timed switches in nonessential lighting areas, such as storerooms. Also, install low-temperature occupancy sensors or timed switches in walk-in coolers and freezers to control lighting.

- **Ensure that dishwashers and garbage disposal units are running only as needed.** Install low-flow pre-rinse spray nozzles on dishwashers to conserve water.

- **Monitor temperatures.** Every degree of cooling increases energy use by 4-5 percent. Stick with 78 degrees for occupied cool, or 68 degrees for occupied heat.

- **Skylights.** Install skylights to provide natural sunlight to illuminate a building's interior.

- **Heat water for hand washing to 110° F instead of 140° F.** Don't reduce the temperature of water serving the dishwasher. Use antibacterial soaps to ensure food safety.

- **Install flow restrictors or aerators in piping and on faucets.** These can reduce water flow by about 50 percent.

- **Insulate new piping.** Insulate and/or repair existing hot water piping and tanks. In a system with about 200 feet of piping, good insulation will save approximately $50 to $75 per year. Also install drain covers on all sink and floor drains (available at www.atlantic-pub.com).

- **Install magnetic disposer-saving products.** For attractive flatware, staples, bottle caps and more, see www.atlantic-pub.com.

- **Repair leaky faucets.** A hot-water faucet dripping

at the rate of 1 gallon an hour consumes 9,000 gallons per year and $50 to $120 in energy. Use faucet-control devices available at www.atlantic-pub.com.

- **Use a motion-controlled water system in the kitchen.** This means that your basin taps automatically turn on when something is placed in front of them. Overuse of water in the prep of food and washing of dishes is unnecessary and costly. A system like this allows you to use water only when it's needed and automatically turns off when it's not.

- **Insulate the water heater tank.** Insulation kits cost very little and will pay for themselves in energy savings in 12 months or less. Follow manufacturer's directions.

- **Use lock covers on thermostats** to ensure tamper-proof temperature settings.

- **Preheat cooking equipment no longer than manufacturer's recommendations.** Turn down cooking equipment when order activity is slow.

- **Solar coatings.** Apply solar "clear" coatings to reduce solar heat from large southern- and western-facing windows.

- **Make sure HVAC economizers are working.**

- **Change all air filters regularly.**

- **Replace worn door gaskets on walk-in coolers and freezers.** Make sure automatic door closers are working. Lubricate refrigerator and freezer hinges and latches. Tighten loose hinges to prevent air leaks.

- **Keep the evaporator fans free of debris.**

- **Ensure that evaporative coolers on air units are well-maintained** and functioning properly.

- **Schedule food preparation wisely.** Cook some items during off-peak periods. Consider whether some items can be cooked by the ovens, fryers or steamers rather than by less energy-efficient range tops, griddles or broilers.

- **Preheating.** Do not preheat steam tables, grills, broilers, etc. If you must preheat, 10-30 minutes is generally adequate.

- **Microwave ovens.** They use significantly less energy than other equipment and can be used for thawing, partially cooking and reheating food.

- **Avoid carbon and grease build-up.** This can make your cooking equipment work harder and use more energy. Purchase Sokof, an approved carbon remover available at www.atlantic-pub.com.

Range-Top Operation - General Energy-Saving Tips

Whenever possible, do not use the range top. Instead, use other equipment, such as steamers and ovens, that use less energy and add less heat to the kitchen. Also:

- **Use the proper-sized pots and pans for individual burners.** Placing a ten-gallon pot on the smallest burner on your stove will consume far too much energy in cooking, while placing a tiny pan on a huge burner will see most of the energy being used completely wasted. Electric burners or heating elements should be at least one inch less in diameter than the pot.

- **Place pots close together.** Placing pots as close as possible on the range top will reduce heat loss and perhaps allow you to turn off a section.

- **Cover all pots.** Covering pots reduces heat loss and causes the food to cook faster. If possible, use glass or clear lids.

- **Turn heat off a few minutes early.** Residual heat in the burner and pot will continue to cook the food.

Range-Top Operation - The Specifics

Make a major impact on reducing range top operational costs. Adopt some (or all!) of the following procedures:

Griddle operation:

- **Preheat griddle** approximately 6 minutes. Six minutes is sufficient preheating time for a 350° F temperature requirement.

- **Heat only a portion of the griddle.** If the griddle can be heated in sections, heat only the sections needed.

- **Cover griddled products.** This reduces cooking

times. It also allows some items to be cooked on one side only.

- **Use griddle weights.** Placing weight on bacon and sausage or other griddled products will shorten cooking time, but may alter the food appearance.

Oven operation:

- **Keep oven doors closed.** Every second the oven door is open, the temperature drops 3-10 degrees.

- **Don't use two ovens when one will do.** Bake products requiring the same temperature in one oven.

- **Don't preheat unless necessary.** Preheating is usually necessary only for baking products.

- **Don't set the thermostat higher than needed.** The oven will not heat up any faster.

- **Don't use aluminum foil.** Wrapping potatoes or other products in aluminum foil retards baking because the foil reflects the oven's heat. If you want to use aluminum foil, wrap the potatoes after cooking.

Fryer operation:

- **Fry from 300-350° F.** Higher temperatures are inefficient. (For older fryers, the temperature may have to be set to 375° F.) Check your manual.

- **Idle the fryers at 200° F.** This conserves up to 50 percent of energy use.

- **Melt fat and oil before frying.** First, bring it to the proper temperature in a steam-jacketed kettle. This is more energy efficient than using the fryer's coils to melt it.

- **Keep fat above coils or elements.** Be sure the fat level is kept above the coils or elements. If they are even partially exposed, 25 percent of the heat entering the fryer can be wasted.

- **Have foods as dry as possible when frying.** A large amount of energy is needed to change water drops or ice on frozen products to steam. Food, such as potatoes and chicken, can be partially cooked by steam and then finished and browned in a fryer.

Steam cooking:

- **Begin cooking procedures in a steamer.** Partially cook your product in a steamer and finish it with your usual cooking method. Remember, steam is the most efficient form of cooking because it cooks moderately, transfers heat rapidly, requires little preheating and shortens cooking time.

- **Cover steam-jacketed kettles.** Clouds of steam indicate unnecessarily high temperatures and put a further load on your ventilating system.

- **Steam tables are energy wasters.** Do not preheat them longer than necessary and turn them off when not in use.

Here are some tips that can significantly trim your dishwasher operating expenses:

- **Air-dry dishes.** Do you really need your dishes to be power-dried at the end of the dishwasher cycle, at all times through the day? During slow periods, or at the end of the night, leave the dishes to air dry, thereby saving energy and reducing your operating expenses.

- **Fully load the dishwasher.** Be smart about the use of the hot-water pre-rinse hose. Heat water only to the temperature required for specific uses within the facility, such as a 140° F supply to a dishwasher.

- **Keep dishwasher temperature at the correct level.** Dishwasher water temperature should be set at the lowest point allowed by local health department guidelines to conserve the energy needed to heat your water. Standard temperatures are: 140° F, wash; 160° F, power rinse; 180° F, final rinse. Using hotter water wastes energy.

- **Save even more electricity by actually turning the dishwasher off when not in use.** Just leaving an appliance switched on for hours at a time costs your business money.

- **Consider substituting chemical rinses for hot-water rinses if codes allow.** A chemical solution such as a bleach-type product could be used instead of 180-degree water for the final rinse.

- **Turn off booster heaters.** Turn dishwasher water

heaters off when the machine is not in use and at closing.

- **Check power rinse.** Make sure that the power rinse on the dishwasher is turned off automatically when the tray has gone through the machine.

- **Clean the dishwasher regularly.** Check wash and rinse jets after each use. Empty the scrap trays frequently. Use a de-liming solution regularly. Lime buildup clogs the wash and rinse jets.

Functioning at Optimum Efficiency

If you want to reduce your kitchen operating costs, getting the most from your equipment is not an option - it is a necessity! Bear in mind the following:

- **Check all thermostats.** Have the thermostats on your ovens checked at least bi-monthly. If your thermostats are off-kilter, you could be using more (or less) gas than you need to, with potentially disastrous results concerning the quality of your meals and your expenses. Check thermostats with a thermometer and adjust them if necessary. Thermometers for all types of kitchen use may be found at www.atlantic-pub.com.

- **Keep gas flames adjusted.** Properly adjusted gas flames should be all blue with a firm center cone. A yellow-orange tip means that some gas is not being burned. There should be no visible smoke.

- **Inspect pipes regularly for leaks.** Hot water and steam leaks are great energy wasters. Replace all valves or gaskets that show leakage. Replace washers in dripping water faucets.

- **Check overheating ovens.** Ovens that become excessively hot on the exterior surface have insufficient or deteriorated insulation, which should be replaced. Also check oven door gaskets for a tight fit.

- **Separate food items into several categories.** This is more energy efficient than storing them all in one large refrigerator. Items should be separated according to the frequency they are needed; store infrequently used items away from frequently used items. For example, beef patties and French fries can be stored together in one refrigerator; other items used less frequently can be stored in another refrigerator. Label items to avoid searching with the door open.

- **Don't set the thermostat below the required temperature.** Though doing this fractionally decreases the freezing or cooling time, it uses significantly more energy.

- **Don't store food in a way that blocks circulation within the refrigerator.** Use several trays so that cold air can circulate around all the products.

- **Kitchen layout.** Locate the refrigeration equipment away from sources of heat, such as ovens and grills. Also, ensure that your stoves, hot plates, microwaves and ovens are located far away from coolers and air-conditioning vents. If your hot plate is being 'cooled' by an air conditioner, you'll be spending more than you need to on gas just to keep it at a level temperature.

- **Are there leaks developing in the seals of your kitchen cooking equipment?** Have your staff on the lookout for steam leaks when you have your pots and pans covered. Of course, steam will escape naturally if a lid isn't fastened, but if it's coming from one spot only and a little too easily, then your lid might be out of shape and allowing energy to be wasted.

- **Keep foil burner trays under the burners.** This saves time in cleaning and keeps your energy focused where it should be – on the food.

- **Place thermometers in refrigerated units and ovens.** Monitor them on a regular basis to make sure all your units are functioning properly and that food is being stored at the correct temperatures. Thermometers for all food service applications may be found at www.atlantic-pub.com.

- **Outlet pipes.** The pipes from your hot water outlet to your dishwasher should be a maximum of 48 inches, from one outlet to the other. If your pipes are running the length of an entire wall, your water will lose heat over the course of that trip and will be far less effective in the wash.

- **Protect your equipment.** Purchase any available protective rails, guards and bumpers for all your equipment. These are generally offered as accessories. They need to be provided both on the mobile equipment and on the fixed equipment you own.

- **Get your hot water back.** Heavy hot water usage warrants consideration of a "heat exchanger" or "reclaimed" to recapture and reuse "waste" heat before it has been truly lost. In a commercial restaurant, heat in the to-be-discarded washing or rinsing water may be recaptured before the water goes down the drain and used to preheat cold water via a "heat exchanger." Whether the investment in the reclamation device is cost-effective depends on the amount of water being used, its "discard temperature" and the cost of installation. Hot gas heat exchangers, installed in the hot gas line (between compressor and condenser), recover heat from refrigeration systems. Water circulates through the heat exchanger, transferring heat directly to where it is used, or to a hot water tank.

- **Rooftop spills and grease.** Contamination generated from exhaust ducts and ventilators cost food service operators thousands of dollars each year. Rooftop grease spills are also a major health and safety hazard. Such grease spills also pose a safety hazard, particularly in relation to slip and fall accidents that, in return, cost thousands of dollars in workers' compensation and personal injury claims each year. See the following Web sites: www.grease-trapworld.com, www.darlingii.com/restaurant/restaurant.htm, www.worldstoneinc.com or www.environmental-biotech.com.

Get the Most from Your Ice Makers

A waste chill recovery (WCR) heat exchanger could be applied to any ice maker in order to improve its energy efficiency. The WCR device is basically a type of "shell and tube" heat exchanger that pre-cools water being charged to the ice maker with cold waste water being discharged from the ice maker. This results in significant energy savings. Contact Maximicer, 13740 Research Blvd., Suite K-5, Austin, Texas 78750, phone 512-258-8801, fax 512-258-8804 or toll free at 800-289-9098. To reach Maximicer on the Web, go to www.maximicer.com or e-mail ice@onr.com. Another good source is Fast Ice Products: Environmental Industries International, Inc., 4731 Highway A1A, Suite 216, Vero Beach, Florida 32963, phone 561-231-9772, fax 561-231-9773 or toll free at 800-373-3423.

- **Pre-chill the water in your ice makers.** Run the water lines for your ice makers through your walk-in cooler to pre-cool the water prior to use.

Waste Management

Effective waste management is one of the best ways to reduce restaurant operating costs. Here are some simple tips:

- **Reduce the volume of waste** that goes into the waste disposal unit.

- **Order items in reusable tubs.**

- **Purchase condiments in bulk** and refill dispensers.

- **Switch to soda and beer dispensers** rather than offering bottles and cans.

- **Use concentrated cleaning agents.**

- **Bulk buy.** This refers particularly to dry foods that can be stored in ingredient bins.

- **Bale and recycle cardboard.** Also recycle plastic bottles and aluminum cans. Recycling isn't only about being environmentally conscious - it also helps you reduce garbage collection expenses and even make a little money on your waste, rather than forking out to have it hauled away. If you sell bottled beer, put any returned recycling deposits towards the price of your next order.

- **Crush and recycle all aluminum cans.** Crushing the cans allows you to place a lot more into a smaller space, greatly reducing the space needed to keep them. You wouldn't throw away the pennies from your cash drawer, so why throw away the pennies each aluminum can will bring?

- **Use pulpers.** Rather than sending all the chopped-up waste out of the drain by using the disposer, pulpers draw waste down into cutters that mince it into tiny bits. The resulting slurry, which is 95-percent water and 5-percent waste, is then forced through a press or extractor. The remaining pulp is discharged down a chute into bags to be placed in a dumpster. See www.insinkerator.com, www.spirac.com.au/products/pre_dewaterer.html or www.go-ami.com/Commodor_AMI.htm.

- **"Gun" dispensers.** Rather than using costly bottles and cans of soda in your drinks, install a gun dispenser that runs from a post mix system. The cost of soda dispensed from these systems is barely a few cents per drink compared with the cost of bottled products, saving you not only a great deal in cost, but also in waste management, spoilage, storage space and delivery.

- **Are your linens, cutlery and glassware walking out with the trash?** Often kitchen staff can take a very cavalier attitude towards what goes into the trash. If only a few pieces of silverware are lost per shift, that quickly amounts to a significant cost to your business. Surveys demonstrate that flatware is the leading item purchased by operators industry-wide. Why? Because so much flatware goes into the trash! Perform occasional inspections of the kitchen trash to ensure you're not letting inventory be thrown away. Use tray savers and magnetic retrievers to keep your trays and silver in service and out of the trash. See www.atlantic-pub.com.

- **Sewerage disposal.** Some cities offer markedly lower sewerage charges if a restaurant uses a pre-treatment waste water system. Contact your local city officials and check if you qualify for any discounts.

Other Great Opportunities to Reduce Costs

The phone, electricity and gas aren't the only utilities where you can make big savings if you're a smart manager. Water, cleaning supplies, postage and trash removal are also areas where you can make big savings. Consider the following opportunities:

- **Renegotiate your credit card discount rates.** This could result in huge savings. A 1-percent discount for a restaurant grossing $1,000,000 per year could result in a $10,000 savings. It pays to shop around when looking for a merchant account provider. Some banks charge high setup fees, whereas others charge no application fees. All merchant account companies charge some type of usage fee. Typically they offer a "discount rate," which ranges from 1-4 percent. There may also be an additional fee for each transaction. In addition, you may also be charged a monthly statement fee of about $10-$20. Negotiate with your bank and contact your state restaurant association - they may have negotiated a lower rate for members. Use comparison services such as www.searchmerchants.com or www.merchantexpress.com.

- **Group and organization dues and discounts.** Review the organizations that your business belongs to and make a list of what discounts, specials and/or promotions you receive in return. If the local chamber of commerce is charging you a membership fee, you should expect a return on that investment that goes far beyond the tea and cookies they put out at the monthly meeting. Ask for promotions to increase local business, discounts from suppliers, community events - anything that will bring you a tangible return. If you don't get what you want, cancel your membership and save the cash for your own marketing.

- **Sell as many gift certificates as possible.** A gift certificate sale is like an interest-free loan from your customer. They give you cash in exchange for a piece of paper that may or may not be redeemed at some future date. In effect, you have free use of their money. Use a computer program such as Giftworks which may be found at www.atlanticpub.com.

- **Table decorations.** Centerpieces don't always have to include fresh flowers, candles and other items that will require ongoing maintenance. Consider using a bowl of water with colored stones and small floating tea candles. These are very inexpensive and the effect can be extremely ambient.

- **Landscaping**. For your exterior landscaping, have perennial flowers planted rather than plain old shrubs. Perennials will flower year after year, they don't need trimming and you will not have the expense of replanting flowers every year.

- **Donations.** When asked to donate to a local charity, offer instead to provide a gift certificate or host the group's meeting in a separate room for no charge. In this way, you will preserve cash and bring people into the establishment.

- **See if your bank will accept quarterly financial statements** from you, instead of requiring monthly numbers as a condition of your loan.

- **Control spending.** As an alternative to departmental budgets, ask people to justify everything they spend.

- **Push for cash discounts.** Many suppliers offer free freight once you hit a certain volume. See if you can bundle orders together to take advantage of the savings. Also, to generate cost-cutting ideas, invite your vendors to a cost-cutting party.

- **Lease equipment.** Consider selling off equipment you currently own and leasing it back. Leasing companies will lease back your existing facility or capital equipment. You would receive cash up front and make periodic lease payments plus interest. There are buy-out options at the end of the lease.

- **Reduce music licensing fees from BMI & ASCAP.** There is a way to receive one low-cost license from these organizations. The national trade association for tavern owners (the National Licensed Beverage Association) recently negotiated a group license agreement covering most of its members, costing

$30 per participating store per year. You automatically become a member of NLBA by joining your state licensed beverage association. See www.nlba.org for more information.

- **Conserve cash and join a barter club.** Barter allows you to buy what you need and pay for it with otherwise unsold products - food and beverages or even catering services - without the use of cash. Almost anything and everything can be purchased with barter services. Nationally, over 250,000 businesses are involved in barter. Check out these Web sites: www.barterwww.com, www.barterbrokers.com or www.netlabs.net/biz/itex/index.htm.

- **Free consulting.** Get the professional advice you need for free. The Service Corps of Retired Executives (SCORE), www.score.org, 202-205-6762, is a network of retired businesspeople who volunteer management assistance. U.S. Business Advisor (www.business.gov) is a government Web site that provides one-stop access to federal information and services.

CHAPTER FOUR

REDUCING FOOD COSTS

Setting Menu Prices

This manual is, of course, devoted to operating costs. However, food costs are such a large part of your expenses that we should at least take a quick review. Here are some important considerations when setting your menu prices:

- **Ideally, it should cost you $0.25 to make every dollar you earn.** This means that once you've established what it costs you to make each meal (including wages, insurance costs, equipment purchase and maintenance and building rental), you should multiply that figure by 3.33 to determine what that item should cost on the menu. Of course, in the real world, costs tend to run higher. In general, restaurant owners and managers try to realize a gross profit of 10-20 percent of total sales.

- **Keep in mind that factors other than direct costs will influence your menu prices.** Indirect factors, such as how a customer perceives quality, your location, the restaurant's atmosphere and the competition, will also play a role in your menu-pricing decisions.

- **You can buy software that will facilitate the costing procedure.** Atlantic Publishing offers one such program called NutraCoster. NutraCoster will calculate product cost (including labor, packaging and overhead) and nutritional content. The program costs about $300 and can be ordered online at www.atlantic-pub.com.

- **Try to price your menu so that the cost price of each meal is 70 percent of the sales price.** In other words, try to price your menu items so that expenses cost about two-thirds of the sale price. If you can bring other expenses down and do a good job of up-selling to your customers, you should be able to make a good profit while providing your customers with great meals at a great price – a win/win situation. Up-selling can be accomplished in a number of ways. Coach your waitstaff on suggestive selling. By having servers ask if a customer wants appetizers or desserts, the customer is more likely to order these extra items.

- **Menu item placement.** Where you place an item on your menu is important in determining whether or not the customer will order the item. Customers are most likely to remember the first and last things they read. By placing the items you want to sell (the items that yield the highest profits) first or last, you increase the chance of selling them. By placing items you want to sell in areas such as these, you are more likely to see them sell. So, place you high-profit/low-cost items in these positions.

- **Change your menu to accommodate large price shifts.** When the price of beef soars, consider raising your main menu prices to accommodate. Change your menu items to use pork, chicken or another meat with an acceptable price level.

Menu Costs

Use your menu as a means for reducing your operating costs:

- **Menu sales analysis.** A menu sales analysis is a good tool to use to track what you are selling. Keeping track of this information will enable you to identify areas where you can reduce costs, such as labor, waste, rising food cost or over-portioning. A menu sales analysis will tell you three things:
  1. How much of a particular item was sold.
  2. The cost of the item.
  3. The profitability of the item.

- **Produce reports.** Many restaurants have computerized cash registers, so getting a report on what items sold nightly, weekly or monthly is easy. If your restaurant does not have a computerized register, you can track a period of time and get this information by pulling it off guest checks.

- **Pull all this information into a simple table so you can compare it easily.** See the example below:

Item	Popularity*	Cost	Menu Price	Profit Margin
Pork tenderloin	42/100	$0.62	$12.50	$4.88
Spaghetti & meatballs	12/100	$1.79	$8.25	$4.46
Shrimp scampi	46100	$3.40	$15.95	$7.55

**42/100 means 42 tenderloins were sold out of a total of 100 entrees served in that time period.*

- **Now what do you do with this information once you have it?** What does this information tell you about how you can reduce costs? Looking at your table, you see that your pork tenderloin is almost as popular as your shrimp dinner, but it costs a good deal less to make. You can summarize that by focusing on such lower-cost items. You can also increase your profit margin by decreasing your food cost. Keep in mind, however, that by only focusing on low-cost items you will lower you guest check average and this will lower profits. To reduce costs and remain profitable, you should emphasize a mix of high- and low-cost food items on your menu.

- **Menu costing software.** There are many software packages available to help you with menu costing. Costguard's Web site, www.costguard.com, offers a product called Menu/Sales Engineering that tracks your sales mix information and provides analysis of your most and least popular and profitable items. The product sells for $495. Calcmenu is another software product you can use for menu costing, inventory management, menu planning and nutrition analysis. You can find Calcmenu at www.calcmenu.com. There are various versions that are priced between $580 and $950. The site also offers a free trial version.

Calculating Food and Drink Costs

The following guidelines will help you calculate food costs for your restaurant:

- **Inventory.** Start by calculating the value of your beginning inventory. Then add your purchase costs over the course of the month. At the end of the month, subtract the value of your remaining inventory from that figure to produce your monthly food expenses. Divide this figure by food revenue for the month and you'll know exactly the food cost percentage of sales.

- **Cost of sales is the cost of the food or beverage products sold.** Food cost of sales is calculated in the following manner:

COST OF SALES — Food	
Beginning inventory	$10,000
Purchases	$90,000
Total	$100,000
Ending inventory	$7,000
Food cost of sales	$93,000
Food Sales	**$250,000**
Food Cost Percentage	**37%**

- **Drinks.** Beverage cost of sales and operating supplies would be calculated in a similar manner. Wine and beer should also be separated into another Cost of Sales category.

Standardized Recipes

Using standardized recipes helps control costs and ensures quality and consistency of menu items. By providing your cooks and bartenders with this necessary information, you can retain control over portioning. Keep these in the kitchen and bar so your kitchen and bar staff will use them. You can store them on index cards and an index cardholder or use a three-ring binder with recipe sheets inserted into transparent envelopes that can be easily wiped clean. Information to include on your kitchen recipe form follows:

- **Name of item and recipe number.**

- **Yield** - the total quantity the recipe will prepare.

- **Portion size** - this may be listed by weight or number of pieces. You may want to include what size of utensil to use for serving. For example, use the 6-oz ladle for a cup of soup.

- **Garnish** - you may want to draw a diagram or include a photograph to show your staff how the item should look when it leaves the kitchen.

- **Ingredients** - make sure to list quantities of ingredients used.

- **Preparation instructions.**

- **Finishing** - describe any finish the product needs, such as brushing with oil or melted chocolate drizzled on top. Also include how to cool and at what temperature the product should be held. Can it sit at room temperature or does it need to be refrigerated?

- **Cost** - include every ingredient and every garnish for accuracy. You will need to look at product invoices to get unit prices, then determine the ingredient cost from this. Total the cost of each ingredient for your total recipe cost. This figure can then be divided by the number of portions in order to arrive at a portion cost.

How to Economize Without Reducing Quality

Try the following food/ingredient cost-reducing tips. They could make a big difference to your overall expenditure.

- **Extend the life of oil or fat for the deep fryer.** By following these six simple steps, you can almost eliminate the need to discard old fry oil or fat:
  1. Thoroughly clean fryer baskets and the fryer elements with a mild detergent rinse at least once a week.
  2. Filter with the Fry-Saver, from www.espresso-plusmore.com, one to three times per day or after each shift.
  3. After one week, remove 50 percent of the filtered oil or fat and store in a clean container to be used for daily "top off" oil.
  4. Refill fryer with 50 percent new oil and continue using.
  5. Add used, aged, filtered oil or fat for upkeep to refill fryer back to fill line.
  6. Repeat steps on a regular schedule.

- **Use air pots for coffee.** They are sealed and insulated like a thermos and can hold temperature and coffee quality up to eight hours.

- **Bread baskets.** The potential for waste in bread baskets is large. Most of these come back from the table partially eaten at best. You may want to consider giving bread baskets only if requested or you may want to cut down on the amount served. You could also consider including packaged items since these can be reused. Some operators are now serving bread only by request and one roll or breadstick served from a bread basket with tongs at a time.

- **Cut kitchen waste.** One of the major culprits in high food costs is waste. Put a new garbage can in the kitchen. This can is for wasted product only, such as wrong orders, dropped food, etc. By giving your kitchen staff this visual aid, you can reinforce the amount of money that gets spent on such product waste.

- **Substitute premade items for some items you have been making from scratch.** You don't have to sacrifice quality, many premade items are particularly high standard. You can also start with a premade item and add ingredients. For instance, you can buy a premade salad dressing and add blue cheese or fresh herbs. Using these items will lower your food and labor cost and you can still put out a quality item.

- **Use industry information.** Check out www.restaurantnews.com/foodcost.html for other restaurateurs' tips on how to lower food costs.

Portion Control

Ensure all employees adhere to portion standards. If the portions your staff is serving are just 10 percent more than you're budgeting for, you're giving away a lot of money every month. This holds true from the size of a slice of meat to the amount of salad and dressing served with each meal. Bear in mind the following:

- **Weights and measures.** Ensure your kitchen staff weighs all portions and ingredients before cooking them so as to meet recipe specifications on every meal. Often when you purchase from suppliers, you're paying by the pound, so if your portions are too large, you're losing money on every meal. Trim where necessary and maintain consistency wherever possible.

- **Established recipes.** Restaurant recipes have two purposes: to ensure consistency and control costs. Following these practices will keep food costs from getting out of control. Also, having a consistent quality for all your meals won't hurt the way your establishment is perceived by customers.

- **No "free handing it."** Be sure your staff is using scales, measuring cups, measuring spoons and appropriate ladles. Often cooks will "free hand it" after a while. This usually results in over-portioning.

- **Does your staff use trim items from meal preparations in other meals?** For example, meat trimmings can be used for soups to great effect, celery leafs can be used as garnishes and pastry off-cuts can be re-rolled and used.

- **Fixed menu.** Maintain a fixed menu for your business, one that allows you to keep a smaller inventory and a fairly simple price list for employees to remember. When you do offer daily specials, fashion them around whatever ingredients you managed to buy for a great price that week, or items in your inventory that you would like to move. If you do use a seasonal menu, try to use local growers for lower produce prices and design seasonal menus that allow you to use ingredients in several dishes so you can order in bulk.

- **Side dishes.** Soups, breads and salads have a far lower fixed per-plate cost than your entrée meals, so make your soups and salads available with a variety of meals and ensure they're of high quality. Your customers will notice how good these meals are, and allow you to keep your entrée portions to a manageable size without leaving customers hungry.

- **Portion out all condiments, sauces and breads according to the number of guests at a table.** If servers put more bread on the table than is needed, your patrons will inevitably eat more and order less. Similarly, if the bread is thrown away and not used, it is simply wasted money.

- **Plate size.** Be certain your kitchen staff uses the correct size dish for each menu item. If they are serving a salad on a dinner plate, they will probably serve too much since the prescribed portion will look small on a large dinner plate.

- **Train your staff.** Have standardized recipes charts and measuring equipment available. Train all new employees and spend time retraining existing staff at regular intervals.

CHAPTER FIVE

PURCHASING & STORAGE

Food Purchasing

Does it sometimes feels like you are constantly ordering food for your restaurant? Where is your inventory going? How much have you invested in the stock room this month? How much did that dropped chicken breast, which was just thrown away, actually cost you? Here are some essential purchasing tips:

- **Consider buying in bulk.** When purchasing food and supplies, always seek to buy in bulk if it can save you money. Items like spices have a very low spoilage rate and can be stored for a long period, without losing quality.

- **However, when you find a great price, don't over-purchase.** A long-term saving may be offset by additional storage costs, spoilage and by having your finances tied up in stock that won't give you a return on your investment for some time.

- **Name brands.** When purchasing food, avoid more expensive "name brands" wherever possible. Of course, you want to make sure you're buying quality ingredients for your food, but are your customers really likely to tell the difference between a name brand as opposed to an industrial brand?

- **Buy local.** Talk to local fresh produce suppliers to see if you can't get fresher, cheaper, better quality fresh produce direct from the grower. Why pay a supplier to get the fruit and vegetables, ship them to their central warehouse, then ship them back to you, when you can just drive 10 minutes down the road and enjoy food right off the tree or vine?

- **Include menu items that are essentially made with similar ingredients to other items on the menu.** For example, a shrimp cocktail and shrimp pasta are two very different meals, but the ingredients are simple, inexpensive and don't take up a lot of storage space. Having five or six other pasta sauces offered likewise loads up your menu with choices, without excessively increasing your inventory. Not only will this allow you to buy in bulk and keep costs down, but it will also lighten the load on your kitchen staff.

- **Test sample.** When considering the purchase of a new food or beverage product, ask if you can test a sample before you make your decision. Not only is free stock always a nice thing to have, but also testing a new item properly is essential if you don't want to deal with unforeseen problems later.

- **Check deliveries.** Who checks your purchase orders when food is delivered to you? If the answer is nobody, then you may well be getting fleeced and not even know it. It's an all-too-common practice either to send more than was ordered, charge a higher price than quoted or under-pack a box.

- **Lists.** The person who handles your inventory counts of food and beverages should also be responsible for creating lists of what needs to be ordered. Keeping the main responsibility of deciding purchasing quantities with the person closest to the inventory assures you won't go overboard with your buying habits.

- **Inventory tracking.** Use custom-made restaurant purchasing and inventory software. With inventory-control software, managers can use a laser scanner, similar to the ones used in grocery stores, to scan bar codes. The software can also be linked to your distributors and you can place your orders electronically, based on the inventory. ChefTec, software for inventory control, recipe, menu costing and nutritional analysis, is available at www.atlantic-pub.com, 800-541-1336.

- **Another Web site of interest is www.foodprofile.com.** This site was established for the collection and distribution of product information for the food industry and is part of an initiative called Efficient Foodservice Response (EFR). Distributors pay to list their products on this site. It provides over 65,000 items and has the most up-to-date product information available, including serving suggestions, nutritional information, cooking instructions and ingredient statements. EFR is an industry-wide effort to improve efficiency in the purchasing process. To find out more about EFR, log on to www.efr-central.com.

- **Failing to stock enough supplies to last you until your next delivery is a big waste of money.** Having to pick up supplies from the supermarket across the street might be an easy fix, but it's also very expensive compared to your normal supplier.

Your suppliers are an aspect of your business that can be of great assistance to you, if you know how to deal with them. Good relationships with vendors can greatly reduce your operating costs. Try the following approach:

- **Do you have poor relationships with your suppliers?** Take the time to talk with your delivery person and order-taker. Try to speak with the same people every time you deal with them and build a relationship of trust.

- **Strike a bargain.** Ask what items they have in stock that are an exceptionally good deal this month, or are of greater quality than normal. Ask suppliers if you can do a deal, if they'll knock a few dollars off an item if you buy a larger quantity, or if they'll throw you a discount (or a bonus) if you settle your invoice early.

- **Do you use fixed orders?** Often a fixed order will see you granted a small discount because it allows the vendor to plan their own purchases accurately. But, if you're buying more than you need over the long run, this deal might cost you more than it saves you. Review all standing orders at least every quarter, reducing or increasing where necessary and keep your inventory at a productive level.

- **Use your suppliers' Web sites.** Many of the larger food suppliers, such as SYSCO, have Web sites on which you can place and track orders. Like SYSCO, they may also have links to current market reports and information on new products. You can visit SYSCO's Web site at www.sysco.com.

- **Do you monitor markets regularly for lower prices?** Perform monthly price checks for food, beverages and supplies. If you spot someone selling cheaper than your supplier, ask them to match the price. A supplier trying to get, or keep, your business may offer discounts, bonuses and incentives that can save you a bundle.

Getting What You Paid For

Keep an eye on the deliveries coming through your back door. Don't pay for other people's mistakes; keep an eye out for inconsistencies, mistakes and outright fraud. Here's how to make sure that you get what you paid for:

- **Never pay for any shipping invoice that has not been signed for by an employee from your establishment.** If nobody working for you is prepared to put their signature on paper to say that a delivery arrived and that it was in the order it was supposed to be, then you shouldn't pay the bill until your vendor can present you with a signed copy of the invoice. In short, if it isn't signed for, it doesn't exist.

- **Let employees know that they're responsible for whatever they signed.** If a box is supposed to contain 20 pounds and only contains 19, that should be pointed out and noted when the delivery first comes in.

- **Deal with inventory immediately.** The longer your inventory sits without being put away where it belongs, the faster it will spoil. Don't let deliveries sit waiting to be properly handled. Ensure they're delivered at a time when your staff has the flexibility to put them away. Never, ever, let deliveries be dropped off early in the morning or when nobody is on duty. Goods sitting on your backdoor step will invariably be stolen or spoiled, not to mention a lure for rodents and bugs.

- **Returns.** Insist that returned or refused items are marked and initialed by the delivery person on the packing slip and then put back on the truck before the driver leaves your establishment. It's far harder to send goods back and be credited for them when they've been sitting in your establishment.

Purchasing and Storage Policies

Make sure you have purchasing and storage specifications in place for your staff to follow:

Specifications should include:

- Specific product information for placing orders.
- Correct storage temperatures.
- Rotation policy for stock.

- **FIFO. Use the "first in, first out" (FIFO) system** for all your inventory products. This ensures that items don't sit on shelves and spoil.

- **Minimize food loss in storage** by keeping frozen foods at 0° F and food in dry storage areas at temperatures around 50° F. Keep food in dry storage, on shelves, at least 6 inches from the floor and the wall. Make sure the staff is storing raw meat on shelves below raw produce; and ensure that fresh fish is being kept on ice in the refrigerator to maintain the proper temperature of 30-34° F.

- **Check expiration dates.** Anything with a suspect date should be refused or sent back.

- **Check scales for accuracy.** How often are kitchen scales checked for accuracy? Your scales need to be checked and calibrated on a weekly basis to ensure complete accuracy so that you are not billed for product you haven't received.

- **Make sure your scales are adequate** to check the weight of incoming orders. You should be able to check, quickly, if you are receiving 50 pounds of hamburger or only 45 pounds. If you don't have scales, consider purchasing them. To purchase kitchen scales online, visit Scale World at www.scaleworld.com, Scale Man at www.scaleman.com or Itin Scales at www.itinscale.com.

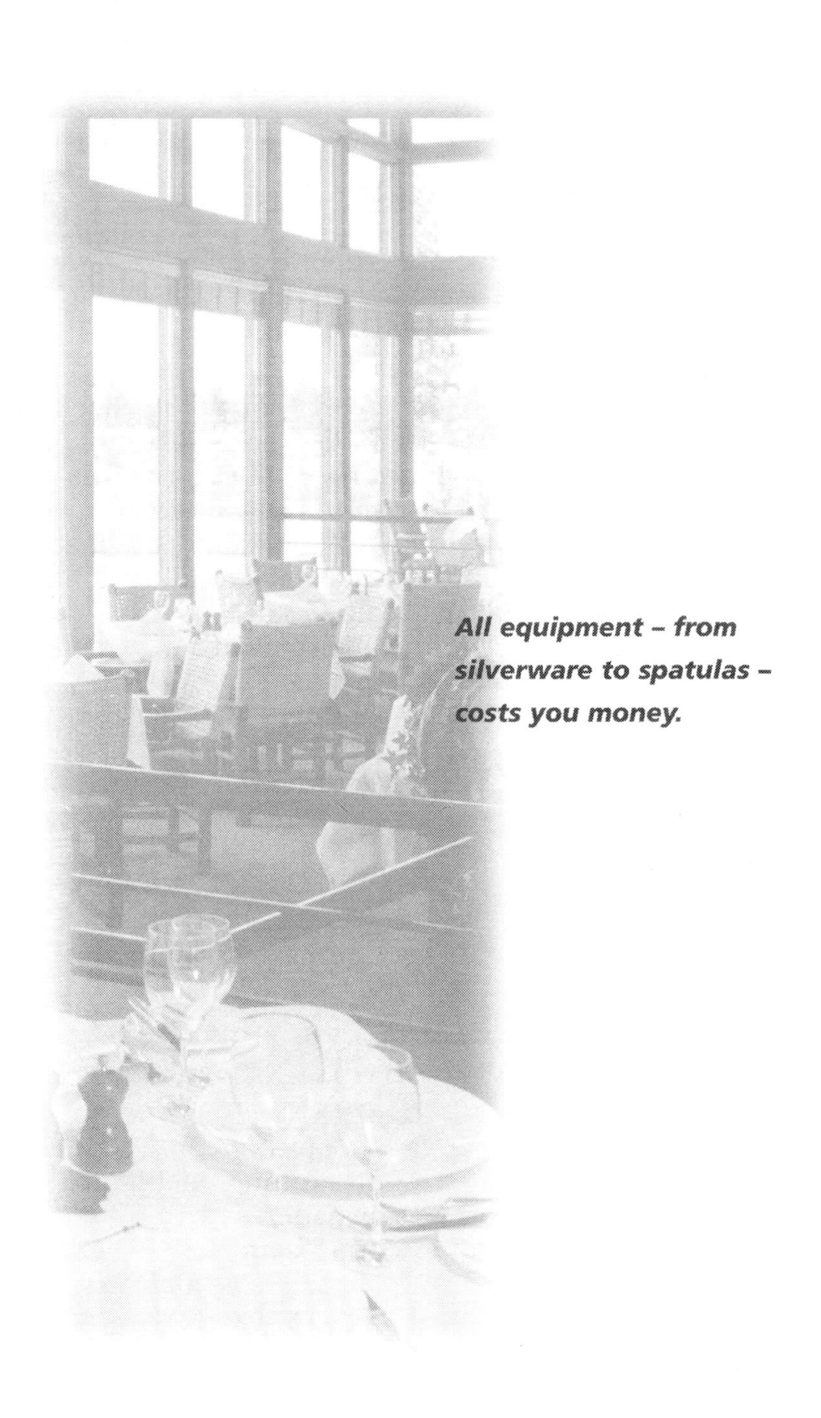

All equipment – from silverware to spatulas – costs you money.

CHAPTER SIX

REDUCING MAINTENANCE & REPAIR COSTS

Linen, Utensils and Equipment

Do you keep inventory of your cutlery, crockery, serving equipment, glassware, napkins, tablecloths, silverware and prep equipment? If no, why not? All of this equipment costs you money. If these items are accidentally thrown out or if every staff member takes a few glasses, a tablecloth, a few plates and some silverware home, you're looking at a huge dollar loss. Also consider the following:

- **How do you take inventory of large quantities of silverware and tableware?** Weigh one spoon, then a bus pan containing all the spoons. Subtract the weight of the bus pan itself and then divide the total weight of the spoons by the weight of one of them. The number you get will be very close to the number of spoons or other silver items you have on hand.

- **Use heat-resistant rubber spatulas and spoons.** New technology has recently brought us flexible scrapers, spatulas and spoons that can take the heat. Up to 400° F without staining, melting or fraying! All items are dishwasher-safe and available at www.atlantic-pub.com.

- **Use recycled products.** If you use paper napkins in your restaurant, consider purchasing recycled paper-based products as a cost-effective, environmentally sound alternative.

- **Are tablecloths really necessary?** Perhaps you'd be better off, financially and aesthetically, in doing without tablecloths altogether. Why not try some elegant reusable placemats instead? Cover the tables in glass and use interesting items such as maps, decorative dried flowers and local memorabilia. Be creative! For example, a sports-themed restaurant might use pennants, baseball cards, etc.

- **Use napkin rings and bands.** Napkin bands or rings save time and money. Put a napkin band around each place setting and set them aside when there is spare time, thus saving labor. It speeds table setting and employee productivity. Napkin bands help you keep the silverware clean and they also help you conform to the rules set forward by the FDA and in developing a HACCP system. Most companies can also customize or print your logo on the band. For a great source, see www.colorkraft.com, 866-382-4730.

On-Premises Laundry

If you currently use a linen service to have napkins and tablecloths cleaned, it might be worth investigating whether it would be more cost effective to set up your own laundry area on the premises. You would need to consider:

- Capital investment dollars
- Operating costs
- Savings and projected pay back of the investment
- Daily and weekly laundry volume in pounds

- Equipment capacity requirements
- Number of operators required to meet expected laundry capacity
- Total daily, weekly and monthly operating costs
- Unit cost per pound of laundry
- Utility consumption information for all machines in the laundry

Employee Uniforms

Your employees' uniforms can cost you a great deal of money. Consider basic black shirts, pants and skirts, for example, that are provided by your employees. Here are some other cost-saving ideas:

- **Aprons aren't only for kitchen staff.** An apron doesn't just keep you're staff from staining their clothes, it also provides a uniform look to your employees and makes them far more noticeable as staff. If you're providing uniforms for your people, supplying an apron to preserve your employees' clothing could save you a bundle in wear and tear.

- **Do you even need to worry about uniforms?** Often a general look can be just as effective as having a uniform, say, for example, requiring all your staff to wear dark blue shirts with black pants, golf shirts with your logo, or even just matching caps.

Janitorial Services

When you're considering your janitorial options, is it better to go with your own cleaning staff, or would it pay to have a professional service come in after hours and give everything the industrial scrub-down?

- **Compare contractors.** The hiring of contract companies to meet your cleaning needs must come only after studying the price and quality of various contractors. Ask yourself how often do you feel that this particular cleaning need must be met in your restaurant. Does this service company have references? Ideally, your expenses for this type of service should not exceed 0.2 percent of your overall sales. If you can find a service that will handle the job at less than your employees' hourly wage rate, grab it!

- **Keep the restrooms clean.** Making sure the restroom has toilet paper and paper towels and that the floors are swept will considerably reduce your janitorial costs. If you can incorporate these jobs into your "general duties" employees' job descriptions, the extra expenses will be minimal.

- **Parking lot.** Keeping your parking lot clean is not as big of a chore as it may sound. At the beginning of a shift, have one of your bussing staff take a broom to collect stray cigarette butts and papers. Having one person do this every day for even just 10 minutes will save you money in your daily operating expenses. Perhaps this will enable you to reduce the use of parking lot janitorial services to once a week.

- **Carpet cleaning.** Consider getting your carpet

stain-guarded. Keep area rugs or runners in the entrance of your dining area so as to pick up water, mud and even snow from ruining your carpet.

- **Cleaning supplies.** To save money on cleaning supply expenses, try using rags instead of paper towels to clean surfaces throughout the restaurant. Paper towels can be very expensive over the course of an entire day's cleaning, while washable rags cost little and can be used again and again. See www.chixtowels.com.

- **When redecorating, pick drapes and curtains that can be machine washed.** This way, waitstaff or management can easily take the window treatments down, have them cleaned overnight and have them re-hung by morning.

Repair Expenses

Always prepare for problems. Repairs are always going to be needed from time to time. Even when you do your utmost to look after your equipment, things break, accidents happen and they can be very costly. So how can you reduce these unavoidable expenses?

- **Maintenance management software.** Use a software program to assist you to schedule maintenance and record the maintenance history and procedures. On the Web, visit www.faciliworks.com, www.expresstechnology.com or www.softwarecorp.com.

- **Downtime.** When a vitally important piece of equipment isn't functioning, it is important to factor into repair expenses the cost of downtime as well as replacing broken equipment.

- **Keep a listing of every piece of equipment you own.** Note the model numbers, brand names, expiration dates and service phone numbers so that when something does break down, you have all the information possible to assist with arranging the service call. It's far cheaper to have enough information at hand for your repair person to figure out a problem with a machine than have him or her come out to see it, go back for a part, then come out again to fix it.

- **Franklin Machine Products (FMP) is the industry leader in parts and accessories for food service equipment.** Need a part for that stove? They've got it. They stock over 8,000 items. Call 800-257-7737 or visit www.fmponline.com. Their annual catalog (thicker than many phone books) is a great resource with many equipment schematics. You'll refer to it often. The staff is very knowledgeable and is known to go to great lengths to access the item you need. Highly recommended, this company will save you money.

- **Consider keeping a handyman on retainer.** Paying a flat $100-$250 monthly fee to a person with skills in the electrical, carpentry, landscaping and plumbing areas is a very cost-effective alternative to hiring specialized contractors in each profession.

- **Timing repairs.** Schedule regular maintenance for the late evening hours or early morning when your establishment is closed or, at the very least, slow. Having to close to perform repairs and maintenance will cost you big in terms of lost business and annoyed, turned-away customers.

Preventative Maintenance

A large part of reducing your yearly repair expenses comes from simple preventative maintenance, planning and forethought. If you and your staff are diligent in the maintenance of your major kitchen and restaurant equipment, it's far more likely to last many years without needing major repairs. This includes your stoves, refrigerators and even freezers. Stick to scheduled cleanings, learn simple small-part repairs and have a serviceman give yearly inspections on all major equipment.

We all know how to dial a phone number and get a repair person to fix a broken appliance, but most businesses fail to realize that preventative maintenance can be a far more cost-effective manner of keeping appliances not just running, but running to peak efficiency. Here's how:

- **Repair manuals**. Read the equipment manuals. Keep them on file for when things go wrong. Quite often a manual will feature advice for cleaning, preventative maintenance and small tips that will save you a service call.

- **Books.** In addition to reading all equipment repair manuals, we recommend you pick up two books for your restaurant. They will pay for themselves on the first use. Both books were written by a veteran restaurant repair person and are available from Atlantic Publishing at www.atlantic-pub.com, 800-541-1336.
    - **"Keeping Your Gas Restaurant Equipment Cooking"** is a handy reference guide that will save time and money; Item #GAS-01, $39.95.
    - **"Keeping Your Electrical Restaurant Equipment Cooking"** covers all types of

electrical equipment, with easy-to-follow directions/instructions; Item #ELE-01, $39.95.

- **Check your ice machine regularly.** Is it working properly? Is there water build-up? Is the machine making more ice than you need and is that ice the right shape to suit your needs? Try to have your water lines run through or past your refrigeration system so that the ice machine doesn't have to work so hard to cool the water.

- **Ensure that your pipes are cleaned regularly.** Dirty or clogged pipes will invariably cause odors and inconvenience that can cost you customers and costly repairs. Make sure that any issues are addressed before they become major problems. Use drain cover baskets for floor drains in the kitchen. They may be purchased online at www.atlantic-pub.com.

- **Schedule the regular cleaning of all equipment as part of your kitchen staffing duties.** While fryers and hoods need to be cleaned more often, the inside of your stoves need scheduled cleaning on a weekly basis, either before or after your regular business hours.

- **Create a checklist outlining maintenance schedules.** Take note of equipment capacities and which items are most likely to break down under stress. A well-maintained kitchen unit will last longer and keep replacement expenses low.

- **Buy a toolbox and fill it with the basic maintenance supplies.** Small and basic repairs can often be performed by management staff or a knowledgeable employee, saving a service call and a great deal of money.

- **Replace burners, handles and timers as needed.** Check these not only for the prevention of food burns and spoilage through improper cooking times and methods, but also to prevent any workers from getting injured on the job, which will save you money on insurance costs.

- **It may seem obvious, but check that any malfunctioning equipment is actually plugged in** before you start calling for service repairs.

- **Web site sources.** For plenty of advice on maintaining your equipment, extending the life of utensils and kitchen remodeling ideas, visit TapDirect: www.tapdirect.com, The Home Store: www.homestore.com, and Leather Man: www.leatherman.com.

Painting Expenses

Your walls do far more than simply keep the roof up. They lend a tone and ambience to your restaurant that can either add to your diners' experience or subtract from it, in a big way. If you ignore your walls for years on end and never count a repaint as an expense, you may well be losing business and gearing up for a major repaint down the road. The following suggestions will keep painting expenses to a bare minimum:

- **Keep up on your in-house painting needs.** Letting your restaurant colors go drab can leave your customers with the feeling that your dining area is unclean or less customer-friendly.

- **When considering using a local painter, ask for references.** While an individual with a brush and ladder can be a very inexpensive option compared with a large painting contractor, a bad paint job can end up costing you a lot of money to fix.

- **Paint.** Consider buying the paint yourself if you are hiring a local handyman for your painting needs.

- **Smoke and grease.** Wiping the smoke and grease from your walls once a month (include the actual dining areas) will keep the paint job fresh and lessen the chances of a repaint being necessary for some time. An additional plus is that clean walls won't smell, leaving your establishment looking and feeling good for your clientele.

- **Web site help.** To save yourself a lot of searching, the Paint Finder Web site, www.paintfinder.com, has a listing of painters available in most areas. Alternatively, check your local Yellow Pages or classified ads in the newspaper.

Liability Expenses

Legal action from a customer, a fire, a catastrophic equipment failure or an employee accident can send your business into financial peril, so it's imperative that you take as many proactive measures to protect yourself. Here are some examples:

- **Reduce the risk of a fire starting in the kitchen.** Keep grease and food from building up within your oven and fry hoods, thereby significantly reducing the chances of a fire engulfing your kitchen.

- **Introduce an in-depth cleaning schedule.** Utilize your labor to its fullest potential and make sure that your business is always in health-inspection order.

- **Inspect your furniture.** Have regular inspection schedules for your furniture as a means not only of keeping your insurance premiums low, but also of reducing the potential for lawsuits filed against your business.

- **Wires and cables.** To reduce the potential for lawsuits, keep your building safe by ensuring all cords and wires are tightly secured and out of the path of anyone walking by. If you must run a wire over a portion of floor space, ensure that it is taped down from end to end and that it is marked with brightly colored tape so that even if someone doesn't spot the wire, they're unlikely to trip over it. If this wire is to be there on a permanent basis, run it along a wall or underneath carpeting.

- **Avoid sharp-edged furniture.** If you're creating a new restaurant, you may want to consider furniture with rounded edges, including tables, bar counters, serving counters and even the cash register.

- **Walk around the exterior of the building.** Does everything appear safe? Check all of your walkways. Could a customer trip easily? Would people with disabilities have problems entering your building? Walk through the interior of the restaurant. Are all the lights working and are they bright enough? Can two people pass between your tables without any trouble?

- **Staff responsibility.** Organize a safety and labor

committee where employees help each other identify the restaurant's "problem areas."

- **"Restaurant Law Basics."** Atlantic Publishing offers a book called "Restaurant Law Basics" that can be an excellent resource for figuring out how to handle situations involving liability. It can be ordered off the Internet at www.atlantic-pub.com. This small investment can save you a lot in legal fees.

Technology Maintenance

Successful restaurateurs realize just what advantages technology can bring to a food operation. By the same token, technology can also hold many traps for the unprepared manager and the costs involved when you make the wrong decisions can prove perilous. Computers crash for no apparent reason. Make sure you can access your information if this happens. Here are some important guidelines:

- **Daily back-ups.** Back up your data daily to another hard drive device, to a remote location, or use one of the many Web-based back-up services such as www.dataprotectionsoftware.com, www.protect-data.com or www.amerivault.com.

- **Printout reports.** Consider having all financial reports printed weekly, or even daily, from your computer. In the event of a major technical crash, these "hard copies" will allow you to keep track of your finances, inventory, scheduling and purchasing and will save you both time and money when things go awry.

- **Manual records.** Consider keeping a Rolodex with your entire collection of important phone numbers, addresses and passwords in case your computer crashes.

- **Payroll.** Ensure that your bookkeeper or office personnel can complete your weekly payroll manually, on paper, so that you do not have to outsource payroll should your computers go down. While outsourcing payroll is an alternative in times of trouble, it could be very expensive for a one-time processing.

- **Listen to your staff.** If your office staff is telling you that a computer, kitchen scale or phone system is not working properly, have the equipment seen to before the problem becomes a large one.

- **Always look for the easy answers first.** Make sure the fax, copier and/or printer has toner, ink and any other necessary cartridges before making a service call. Sometimes a problem with a small electronic appliance could be as simple as having a surge protector switched to the "off" position.

- **Ink jet cartridges.** Since almost all ink jet printer cartridges are refillable, you can purchase refill kits rather than incur the high cost of replacements. Costs of black ink can be as low as 40 cents per refill versus $18 for an ink jet cartridge.

- **For helpful hints on maintenance, try the following sites:** Ask An Expert at www.askanexpert.net or About.Com at pcsupport.about.com/cs/pcmaintenance.

When a table gets a shaky leg, what do you do? Throw it out? Hire a repair person? Whichever you choose, you could be throwing away good money after bad, not to mention damaging the customer experience. While you shouldn't take short-cuts, nor should you pay through the nose. Here's how:

- **Table wobbling?** Nothing is worse than sitting at a wobbly table: it is hard to eat, distracting to talk and beverages get spilt. There are two solutions: wobble wedges and super levels. Wobble wedges are small, clear, angled leveling devices that basically take the place of all those sugar packets you see on the floor. Super levels screw into and replace the existing table feet. Both systems are highly effective. They are available at www.atlantic-pub.com, 800-541-1336, (wobble wedges, Item #WW-01; and super levels, Item #SL-12).

- **Spare furniture.** Keep a couple of extra chairs and tables in storage in case you have need of a replacement in the future. When you buy in quantity, you should see a discount on your purchase price, which creates a savings on the price of the furniture and allows you to maintain uniformity in your furnishings, and make replacement costs a non-issue for a long time to come.

- **Invest a few dollars in scratch-repair polish.** This is an easy and effective measure to keep up with the wear and tear on your dining furniture and the overall appearance of your restaurant. For a host of ideas and tips on do-it-yourself repairs, visit Refresh Furniture at www.refinishfurniture.com or Furniture Wizard at www.furniturewizard.com.

Safety Procedures

Ensuring your patrons and staff aren't injured on the premises is more than a matter of caring for their well-being, it's an essential part of avoiding a business-threatening lawsuit and lengthy downtime. Labor savings, insurance savings, workers' compensation reductions and sick pay savings, not to mention staying out of civil court, all come from putting safety procedures in place - and sticking to them. Here's how:

- **Keep equipment in working order.** Make sure that equipment, tools, machinery and substances are in safe condition.
- **Talk to your workers about safety in the workplace.** Encourage open discussion.
- **Hygiene.** Maintain safe and hygienic facilities including toilets, eating areas and first aid.
- **Staff training.** Offer information, training and supervision for all workers.
- **Involve your staff.** Implement processes to inform workers and involve them in decisions that may affect their health and safety at work.
- **Safety procedures.** Implement processes for identifying hazards and assessing and controlling risks.
- **Accident book.** Record work-related injuries and illnesses.
- **Be observant.** Pay attention to safe work. Your business will not only become more competitive,

but you can help stop the pain and suffering from workplace injury or fatality.

- **Post safety signs.** Ensure safety signs, usually available for free from your local Department of Health or Labor or your appliance manufacturers, are posted about your kitchen. These will include details on how to lift heavy items safely, directions on proper signage for slippery floors and dangerous equipment as well as rules on who handles jobs like lighting gas pilots, changing light bulbs and sharpening knives. Some signs can be downloaded from www.restaurantbeast.com.

Basic Knife Safety

A study by the National Safety Council says hand lacerations cost employers an average of $3,337 in expenses and lost productivity. Yet, so much can be done to avoid both the personal and financial pain involved. Consider the following possibilities:

Keep knives sharp and handle them carefully:

- Don't cut with the edge toward you or your fingers.
- Don't leave sharp knives loose in a drawer.
- If you're working with or handling a knife and you drop it, stand back. Let it fall, don't try to catch it.
- If you have a dirty knife, don't toss it in the dishwater. You don't want the dishwasher to come up with a handful of sharp knifes.
- Don't lay a knife down with the edge pointing up.

- **Gloves cost about $15 per hand.** Knit-type cut-resistant gloves give greater levels of dexterity and comfort. They are made with fabric reinforced with a combination of strong fibers including stainless steel. Metal mesh gloves, made of double-interlocked welded rings (think of a suit of armor) are used by butchers, meat processors, chefs and ice carvers. They provide the highest level of cut resistance. Gloves are available at www.atlantic-pub.com.

- **Knife handling.** Videos and books are available on knife handling and safety at www.atlantic-pub.com.

Tips for a Burn-Free Kitchen

Steam, oil and grease, boiling soups, hot grills and ovens can all result in workplace burn injuries. The Burn Foundation has found that such injuries tend to occur when managers don't enforce safety rules or when workers themselves are careless about safety. The potential for accidents is also greater when workers are worn out, on drugs or alcohol, or are simply taking unnecessary risks. Every restaurant is fast-paced and generally congested, providing all the needed ingredients for a disaster. The following tips can make a big difference to maintaining a burn-free kitchen:

- **Gloves.** Wear protective gloves or mitts when handling hot pots or cooking with hot, deep-frying oil.

- **Footwear.** Wear non-skid shoes to prevent slipping on wet or greasy tile floors.

- **Nip small fires in the bud.** Extinguish hot oil/grease fires by sliding a lid over the top of the container.

- **Hot oil.** Never carry or move oil containers when the oil is hot or on fire.

- **Avoid reaching over or across hot surfaces and burners.** Use barriers, guards or enclosures to prevent contact with hot surfaces.

- **Equipment instructions.** Read and follow directions for proper use of electrical appliances.

- **First aid.** Keep first-aid kits readily available and make sure at least one person on each shift has first-aid training.

- **Keep fire extinguishers accessible and up to date.**

- **"AWARE."** The National Restaurant Association's Educational Foundation offers an educational program called "AWARE: Employee & Customer Safety." The nine modules offered include sections on ensuring fire safety in the kitchen and preventing burns. The Educational Foundation also offers videos that promote workplace safety, which focus on how to prevent on-the-job injuries, along with an interactive CD-ROM.

Other Avoidable Kitchen Hazards

However busy you are, you simply cannot afford to ignore the following danger zones:

- **Hot oil.** Transporting hot waste oil from the fryer is very dangerous. Very serious accidents have occurred as the night crew changes the oil at the end of the shift. They are tired and want to go home and may be rushing. Consider purchasing a Shortening Shuttles®, www.shortening-shuttle.com, 800-533-5711. These inexpensive devices make hot-oil transfer safe and easy and virtually eliminate the dangers and liability of exposure to hot-oil burns.

- **Wet floors.** Ensure anyone mopping a floor area puts out ample signage to indicate the floor is wet and may be slippery. This doesn't mean a single yellow cone; it means enough signage so that a person has to make an effort just to get to the slippery floor.

- **Coolers.** Keep any heavy coolers or storage fridges located at or above waist level, wherever possible.

- **Keep your food supply safe.** Make sure your employees are trained in food service sanitation. Check with area community colleges for courses in food safety and sanitation. The National Restaurant Association also offers ServSafe certification courses through Atlantic Publishing at www.atlantic-pub.com.

HACCP (Hazard Analysis Critical Control Point)

Have a HACCP system in place. HACCP was developed by NASA about 30 years ago to keep astronauts' food supply safe. Until recently, HACCP was almost exclusively used in food production plants, but restaurants are beginning to adopt this approach to food safety. Having a HACCP system in place could save you a fortune in liability costs. If a situation arises, you may be able to prove you were using reasonable care and this can go a long way in a liability suit. Here's how it works:

- **HACCP uses seven basic principles.** Basically, these principles indicate that you need to identify all the critical points at which food can become unsafe, such as during cooking, storage and production.

- **Then you must put measures in place to ensure food remains safe.** These measures can include actions such as establishing minimum cooking times for menu items and having policies about how long food can remain at room temperature before it must be thrown away.

- **Monitoring.** Additionally, you must establish methods to monitor that these policies are being followed.

- **Corrective procedures**. You must also establish corrective actions if the safety measures have not been used.

- **Further information.** For more information on HACCP, HACCP checklists and HACCP form templates, log on to the Food Safety, Education and Training Alliance's Web site at www.fstea.org/resources/tooltime/forms.html.

Common Food-Handling Problems

It is vital that food be handled correctly in your restaurant. Pay particular attention to the following areas:

- **Sink-side nail brushes missing or not used.** Order nail and hand brush kits at www.atlantic-pub.com.
- **Gloves.** Failure to change protective gloves between tasks.
- **Sanitizing surfaces.** Work tables and cutting boards not properly sanitized between uses.
- **Food exposure.** Food exposed for long periods and food such as flour and sugar stored in open containers.
- **Improper delivery procedures.** Deliveries left out too long before being put away. Food delivery boxes picked up from the floor and unpacked directly on to tables.
- **Equipment.** Equipment not properly cleaned.
- **Restrooms.** Empty soap and towel dispensers in restrooms.

Restaurant Hygiene and Safety Issues - Online Info

There are numerous Web sites that can really help you get to grips with restaurant hygiene and safety issues. Here are some sites that provide tips on food service hygiene and safety:

The Minnesota State Department of Health
www.health.state.mn.us

MSU's Insight Into Safety
healthed.msu.edu/student/cteam.html

U.S. FDA Center for Food Safety and Applied Nutrition
vm.cfsan.fda.gov/list.html

U.S. Department of Agriculture's Food Safety and Inspection Service
www.usda.gov/fsis

Gateway to U.S. Government Food Safety Information
www.foodsafety.gov

Bad Bug Book
vm.cfsan.fda.gov/~mow/intro.html

Safety Alerts
www.safetyalerts.com

E. Coli Food Safety News: MedNews.Net®
www.MedNews.Net/bacteria

Safe Food Consumer
www.safefood.org

Food Safe Program
foodsafe.ucdavis.edu/homepage.html

International Food Safety Council
www.nraef.org/ifsc/ifsc_about.asp?level1_id=2&
level2_id=1

The Burn Foundation
www.burnfoundation.org

Your staff can be your best asset.

CHAPTER SEVEN

STAFFING & MANAGEMENT

Make the Most of Your Staff

Your staff can be your most valuable commodity - and also your greatest problem. A productive, skilled work crew can turn your eatery into a thriving success, but, unfortunately, sometimes you will have problems with staff. These problems can range from anything between nonproductivity and criminal behavior. The key factors that affect your employees and their overall productivity in your business include the selection process, training, supervision, scheduling, equipment, morale and your own expectations. Also, to make the most of your staff, try the following :

- **Involve your employees.** Almost all of your employees will have no idea about what it costs to operate a restaurant. Most employees probably think you're operating a gold mine. Keep them informed and they will soon change their attitude. They will then find it easier to rationalize carelessness, waste and theft.

- **Training new employees.** How do your new employees learn your processes when they start working for you? Do you have training material for them to take home and learn or do you rely on other crew members to take time out of their schedule to teach them? What is your training program? A little preparation now can save you big dollars for years down the track. When you hire a new staff member, have written copies of job responsibilities and company policies so the new person knows what is expected of them. For a complete resource of training videos, posters, tools, books and computer software, see www.atlantic-pub.com.

- **Employee satisfaction surveys.** Employee satisfaction surveys can give you a great deal of information, including ways to reduce expenses and keep employees happy. You can distribute employee satisfaction surveys in payroll envelopes and have them returned anonymously, or not. Implement as many suggestions as you can which will result in happy employees, who will, in turn, make your customers happy. The following three Web sites provide templates, forms and Internet service for employee satisfaction surveys, customer surveys and market research: The Business Research Lab at www.busreslab.com/consult/empsat.htm, CustomInsight.com at www.customisight.com or Quask at www.quask.com.

- **Avoid employee dissatisfaction.** Fact: you will experience greater staff turnover if your employees are not happy. This will lead to an increase in your hiring and training costs. A good way to keep your employees satisfied is to keep them informed and feeling like part of the team. When budgets allow, consider throwing them a party, or start a softball team and compete with other area restaurants. Show the employees you appreciate their efforts and hard work; it will go a long way in helping to keep your staff's morale high.

- **Enlist the aid of employees by soliciting suggestions on cost reduction.** Many companies have generated significant savings using this approach. To encourage participation, consider implementing a bonus program based on a percentage of costs saved. However, be wary of "quick fixes" that will have no impact, or worse, prove costly in the long run.

- **Make your staff aware of what equipment and repairs cost you.** Some employees have no idea that a new combination oven might cost as much as a new Jaguar automobile.

- **"Show me the money."** Demonstrate to your employees the reality of the restaurant business. Place a $100 stack of dollar bills on a table. This represents the monthly sales. Then start paying the bills: $32 to the food vendors, $20 for liquor vendors, $30 for payroll, $6 for payroll taxes, $5 to the utility companies, $4 for rent and so on until there are four or five dollars remaining.

Watch for Employee Warning Signs of Substance Abuse

Look for employee substance abuse. In most instances, an employee will need extra money, and the easiest place to look may be your business. According to the U.S. Department of Labor, an estimated 14.8 million Americans are current illicit drug users. Also, nearly 11 percent of youths between the ages of 12 and 17 are current illicit drug users. Among this population, marijuana is the most prevalent drug.

Young adults between the ages of 18 and 20 have the highest rate of current illicit drug use at roughly 20 percent. The rate of current illicit drug use is higher among men (8.7 percent) than women (4.9 percent). In addition, heavy drinking occurs most frequently among young adults between the ages of 18 and 25 (13.3

percent), peaking at age 21 (17.4 percent). Heavy drinking correlates strongly with illicit drug use. Of 12.4 million heavy drinkers, 30.5 percent are also current illicit drug users. What are the warning signs? Look out for the following:

- **Employees who refuse to go on vacation.** They may be afraid that their substitute will discover their dishonesty.

- **Condoning dishonesty.** Some employees who pilfer, steal and even embezzle have developed a different belief system when it comes to theft.

- **Drastic changes in behavior.** Watch for sudden and unexpected changes in employee attitude, mood swings, nervousness, hostility and general behavioral changes.

- **Overprotection of work records, personal file, guest receipts, valet tickets, etc.** Employees who are reluctant to give up the control may be keeping incriminating facts concealed.

- **Intentionally violating work rules.** Employees who rebel against company policies and procedures should be watched because they have no regard for you or your business. Employee embezzlement can put you out of business.

Active Management

No matter what, if management doesn't demonstrate a high level of concern over the rules and procedures that you've set in place, your employees won't either. The "do as I say, not as I do" form of management does not work! Management should not only be heard, but also be seen showing the staff how things need to be done. This involves an almost constant "floor" presence. Here's how to demonstrate active management:

- **Get out of the office.** Walk through the restaurant and watch the way things operate. Learn about your employees, what they are doing, who deals well with customers and how they are going about their daily routines.

- **Lend a hand.** If food is slow coming out of the kitchen, jump behind the line and help. Show your workforce that you are serious and that you are not afraid of hard work.

- **Supervise your host or hostess.** Make sure he or she is aware of the workload on each server's station, seating customers accordingly. This doesn't always mean seating each station equally, as large parties are often more time-consuming for the server than several small parties.

- **Have your employees check the restrooms hourly.** Insist that they mark off a checklist on each trip. Is every aspect of it clean? An unkempt bathroom is something that drastically alters customers' perception of your establishment, while a spotless bathroom will allow them to concentrate on how good your food is.

- **Train servers to please.** Management should have a well-written, established plan on what they can do to please a guest and this should be shared with every employee in the restaurant. A complimentary round of coffees, meal discounts, free drinks and desserts can make a customer's day, but your servers need to know how far they can go without hurting your bottom line.

- **Train servers to thank guests.** It's the responsibility of management to remind all employees to thank guests for visiting your restaurant. Work to ensure repeat customer visits by going above and beyond the call of duty for the customer.

- **Product knowledge.** Management needs to ensure that all employees know exactly what every item on the menu is and how it's prepared. They must also be instructed to pronounce and spell every item correctly. While this may seem obvious, a misunderstanding can prove expensive and embarrassing when a customer receives the wrong order.

- **Enforcement.** Is your current management enforcing the procedures you've implemented? Adherence to the rules and regulations starts at the top. If your employees feel that you and the managers are not enforcing the policies and procedures, then they also will not place an importance on fulfilling your requests.

- **Resolving disputes.** In the event of a dispute with a customer, management should realize that their attitude can turn off a regular customer to your establishment entirely. When a problem arises, ask the guest what they want you to do to solve the problem and, if at all possible, take immediate action. Give a discount, offer a new item, pacify the customer.

- **Review working schedules.** Delegate a senior member of staff or the manager to look over all schedules and suggest any changes based on up-times (or slow times) that they feel need addressing. When you have studied a schedule or spreadsheet long enough, it is easy to overlook obvious problems. For free software and ideas on scheduling, check ZDNet's reviews of management software at www.zdnet.com/downloads/business/employee_management.html.

Time Controls

Using time wisely is an essential part of running a profitable food and beverage operation. Utilizing time controls will create savings in labor costs, customer-waiting times and getting the most productivity possible out of your available tables. Here are some tips for streamlining procedures:

- **Staff responsibilities.** Set up clear responsibility guidelines for all managers and employees to ensure that everyone knows exactly what's expected of them. If your staff is neglecting certain tasks, create extra levels of middle management so that everyone is responsible not only for his or her own job, but also for ensuring others do their jobs too.

- **Scheduling labor.** Complete weekly schedules for your employees with a view to making the schedule suit your incoming customers, not your employees' lives. While this is good advice, restaurant schedules are often a nightmare for the person responsible for making them. Not only does this person have to take into consideration factors such as peak business hours and advertising schedules, but he or she also has to work around class schedules, schedules for other jobs and kids' school activities. It's just a hard fact of the restaurant business that many employees do have other responsibilities that have to be considered.

- **Scheduling software.** Atlantic Publishing offers a software program that can alleviate some of these scheduling headaches. "Employee Schedule Partner" is a software program that can schedule an unlimited number of employees and positions, track employee availability and track payroll. It is available for $295.95 and can be purchased at www.atlantic-pub.com.

- **Make new probationary staff floaters.** Let them know that if things are slow, they'll be sent home early. This won't just save on wages, it will also save on tax expenses, while giving you the flexibility in your labor schedule to cover if the restaurant suddenly gets busy. It may be worth considering sending other staff home early during slow times.

- **Delegate.** When your own schedule becomes crowded and difficult to control, don't be afraid to delegate tasks to your managers. Some people feel that they're losing control when they have others help them with their work, but the real loss of control comes when you can't get your tasks completed in good time.

- **Analyze problems as they happen.** Implement the means to avoid those problems from reoccurring. Think of checks and balances that you can put in place to ensure future problems of this kind are double-checked or confirmed by another employee.

Keeping Staff Efficient

Employee costs can always be trimmed. However, maximizing your staff efficiency must be your first step in keeping costs down if you care about maintaining quality levels with your customers. It can be a tricky balancing act, but it must be an ongoing process within every restaurant business, especially because of the high staff turnover rate in the hospitality industry. As an owner, make your demands known. Don't forget to outline your control measures, policies, rules and procedures during the hiring process of your employees. Also, bear in mind the following issues:

- **Training for all.** Commit yourself to job training - training for yourself, your management and all of your employees. At one time or another throughout the growth of your restaurant, everyone will need to perform tasks that might fall outside the scope of their regular job. An employee trained in multiple skills is a much more valuable fit for your business in times such as these. See www.atlantic-pub.com for all your training needs.

- **"Game face."** When an employee is smiling, not only does the customer feel more welcome, but the act of smiling also makes the employee feel more confident about themselves and their duties. Staff should be encouraged to keep their "game face" on throughout their shift and should be reminded that a smiling server is more likely to be tipped well.

- **Listen.** Listen to servers, cooks, bartenders and even busboys when they express complaints, suggestions and comments. Employees will tell you when something is wrong in the restaurant. They may open your eyes to some important issues that require your immediate attention.

- **Employee personal problems.** The personal troubles of employees will undoubtedly enter your business from time to time. Down time for personal issues may seem like an unacceptable loss for your bottom line, but consider the alternatives - forcing a depressed employee to come to work regardless may well translate to others becoming involved in the problem, or customers catching their "vibes." Sometimes it's best just to choose your battles and encourage a valuable staff member to sort out their problems away from the workplace.

- **Set performance standards for your staff and managers.** Post them for all to see. This way, if a job goes unperformed, there can be no excuses as everyone knows who should be doing what.

- **Employees should be taught not to judge guests.** They should respect all guests and treat them equally. Whether an employee likes a customer is largely irrelevant, rather turning that customer into a "repeat customer" is of paramount importance.

Provide Incentives

Your employees will usually do what you ask for the wage that you pay them. But, if you want them to go above and beyond, sometimes it's a good idea to throw an incentive or two their way. An incentive will cost you a small amount, but if it has your employees all working that much harder, your return will be exponential. Here's how:

- **Recognition.** If you find that breakages in the kitchen or bar area have decreased, then give your employees some recognition for doing a great job. When your employees are happy, they are more apt to relate that happiness to your customers.

- **Make each employee accountable for his or her own individual work.** If a hostess manages to keep "walk-aways" to a minimum during busy times when no tables are available, reward her with a wage bonus or let her go home early during a slow time.

- **Provide your employees with the tools to do their jobs well.** Different employees will have a lot of use for calculators, pens, aprons, tray stands, ample supplies of menus, top-quality food prep equipment and paging systems. Providing employees with needed equipment will help keep morale up and frustration levels down!

- **Reward employees for perfect attendance.** For example, give the employee a free meal coupon for a complete month without their calling in sick or showing up late for work.

- **Provide incentives** for employees who offer

solutions for problems or who will take on additional workloads, thereby raising labor productivity. Consider rewarding employees with preset percentages involving the savings of overtime costs or other repair expenses that you would have incurred had the problem not been not solved.

- **Selling incentives.** Organize selling contests for your servers.

- **Throw a party!** Pick a month to have the entire staff work to lower food cost. If you're running a 38-percent food cost, tell your employees you want to try to lower it to 35 percent that month. Give them an incentive - throw a party at the end of the month if the goal is achieved. Create T-shirts and prizes to give away at the party.

Hiring New Staff

Many hospitality managers find that one of the most difficult tasks in their job is finding the right people to join their staff. Classified ads will certainly bring you applicants, but the best hospitality people are generally not unemployed - they're already working for your competition. The following tips will help you secure the best staff available within the hospitality trade:

- **Your existing staff can be a great source of new staff.** They usually know plenty of industry colleagues that would be a nice fit. A personal reference from someone you respect sure as heck beats a cattle call. Beware, though, of forming "cliques."

- **Keep potential employees on file.** When

someone makes an application for employment and you don't have a spot open, keep that application on file! If they walked in looking for a job when no job was being advertised, you can bet they already know and like your establishment and truly want to work there.

- **Time is money.** Don't waste too much time interviewing everyone who applies for a job. If an applicant isn't to your initial liking, thank them for their application and move on to someone who is.

- **Look for stable personalities when enlisting new employees.** It's traditionally thought that the more stabilizing factors in a person's life - such as having a mortgage or being married with children - the less likely that person will be to leave suddenly or jeopardize their job through tardiness.

- **Try some of the hospitality Web sites for employees.** The sites www.restaurantbeast.com, www.restaurant.org and www.acfchefs.org all have pages for resumes.

- **Area culinary programs.** Check with area schools for potential candidates. These people will already be partially trained for you!

- **What are you looking for exactly?** Different roles require different skills and while not every position requires abundant experience, every position does require a mix of stability, intelligence, personality, honesty and a willingness to work. If an inexperienced applicant shows these qualities, look past any lack of skills and make an investment in a quality human being by training them.

- **Every employee in the public eye is a reflection of your corporate personality.** So it's important that they view every customer as a potential friend, not an irritation. Certain people can light up a room with a smile and if you can find two or three of those people, your customers will be back.

- **Never interview an applicant when they've just made their application.** Make them show how enthused they are by calling them back for an appointment on a later date. If they can't make it, or don't show up, you're better off without.

- **When interviewing potential employees, it's easy to forget important questions.** If you want to be sure you have all the information you require from each person, put together a list of questions in advance. This will allow you to get comfortable, focus on the answers and stay on target.

- **Don't be afraid to ask for a demonstration.** If a prospective bartender has trouble uncorking a bottle of wine or a waitress can't handle four plates at once, it's better that you find out ahead of time.

- **Keep a list of all employee phone numbers on hand in your office.** Include those that have recently resigned on good terms so that when you have an exceptionally busy evening or event coming up, you can find emergency help that knows your business inside out.

Training

All too often, restaurant operators hire employees with certain skills without ever seeking to expand upon them. An employee will rarely object to being taught a new skill. The return on your investment can be substantial when your crew has the flexibility to cover each other's positions. The following training suggestions could make a major impact upon the efficiency of your restaurant - and the happiness of your staff:

- **Always have a manager present training procedures to new employees.** If you leave the training to an existing staff member, you may be unconsciously introducing bad habits to your new employee. Most employees learn little shortcuts they can get away with in their daily duties ("don't bother cleaning under there, nobody ever looks there anyway...") and if you allow your employees to pass these shortcuts on to new people, they become ingrained.

- **Multitasking**. In the long run, it will be to the benefit of both your staff and your establishment if you can train your employees to cover multiple job disciplines. If your bar staff can be trained to take orders, seat customers, clear tables and serve food to a high degree of proficiency, then any time your regular staff are unavailable or busy, your other staff can step in. Alternately, if your floor staff can prepare drinks during a busy period at the bar, it can only help your serving process.

- **Train, re-train and then test.** It isn't enough to tell your staff once what you expect of them and then assume that they understood perfectly. When your employee is trained in an area of the job, revisit that training a few days later to ensure that they totally understood.

- **Streamline your meetings.** Plan for brevity (5-10 minutes). Focus on clear objectives and give participants the background information in advance. Involve only essential decision-makers.

- **Are your dishwashers trained to keep busy during their entire shift?** Save money by giving your kitchen-hands additional duties, such as peeling potatoes, sweeping at the end of the night, aiding the bussers in the disposal of waste, cleaning of the general kitchen area - there are many chores with which they can always assist. Multitasking allows all of your staff to help each other work more efficiently and avoids periods where you're paying a staff member to wait for something to do.

Staff Productivity

Above all, managers must set the example as valuable team players and coaches, not bosses that lock themselves in the office. You should demonstrate that compensation and work ethic are directly related. Managers who are willing to work alongside their team can contribute directly to productivity while building respect and morale. Also consider the following staff productivity issues:

- **Clocking-in times.** Don't allow employees to clock in any earlier than 5 minutes prior to a shift, unless specifically asked to do otherwise. When an employee continually clocks in early, they are accumulating unscheduled hours that will cost you big over the long run.

- **Time cards.** Any time an employee is asked to stay late, the shift manager should sign their time card and list, in a log, what the additional time was used for. This will allow administration to track overtime easily, noting where additional human and financial resources may need to be allocated down the road.

- **Reduce ordering errors.** Train your waitstaff to repeat orders back to the customer. This ensures that guests receive exactly what they ordered and helps to eliminate misunderstandings, mistakes, time and food waste.

- **Regular break times.** Your employees cannot work at top speed for an entire 8-hour shift without getting worn down and making errors. To keep them on top of their game, schedule ample break times, with time for a full meal to recharge both their physical and mental abilities. Yes, this is an added expense for your business, but days off due to stress and tiredness cost you far more. Customers lost due to employee errors and bad attitude is an even bigger hit to your bottom line.

- **Sick and vacation days.** Sick days and vacation days for full-time staff can be difficult to schedule, as you rely on these key employees. Remember that a long-term employee who has accrued such benefits has done so by giving a lot to your business and their value is far greater than the inconvenience of having to replace them when they take time off. To minimize the effect of time off, offer your staff an extra day or two if they take their vacation at more convenient times.

Staff as an Asset

A few subtle techniques can see your serving staff progress from trusty employee to "star of the floor." In fact, quite often the impression your servers leave will be the lasting impression a customer takes away from their dining experience. Try the following techniques:

- **Make sure that serving and hosting staff see themselves as far more than "just" restaurant workers.** In fact, your servers are not only the front line when it comes to interaction with your customers, but they're also the best positioned to read the mood of the room and point out any glitches in the customer experience. Let your serving people know that they control the floor and that if something is amiss, it's as much their job to take care of it or let somebody know as it is a manager's.

- **A good crew of truly professional staff is well worth keeping.** An average server can handle up to four tables at a time, but many "true professionals" can take five or six tables at once - or more! Keep an eye on your servers and always encourage them to expand their skills through positive encouragement, financial incentives and pride in their job.

CHAPTER EIGHT

SECURITY & THEFT PREVENTION

Reducing Employee Theft

Sometimes the best way to improve your bottom line doesn't include making cost reductions, it involves keeping a better eye on money you've already made. Theft reduction is an incredibly important area to keep an eye on, as one sticky-fingered employee can cost you big. Internal theft is a massive area of expense in many businesses, and, though you don't want to spend more on security and precautions than you save, an ounce of prevention is worth a lot of cure. To keep employee theft to a minimum, you'll need to concentrate on the following areas of your establishment:

- **Staff rotation.** If practical, try to rotate your employees so that they are not working with the same people constantly, minimizing the opportunities to collude and steal from the business.

- **Routine inspections.** Using daily inspections is much more likely to spot an employee being dishonest or a system that isn't working well than waiting for a catastrophe to happen. Have management conduct regular surprise inspections throughout the facility, with a view to becoming more aware of what's going on throughout the premises.

- **Watch the bar area.** You can tell if money is being spent or not. If you don't see money being exchanged, it's a safe bet that your bartender is giving free drinks. Reduce your bar expenses by keeping a watchful eye, perform spot register checks at unexpected times. Also, don't allow underage persons to work or be seated around the bar area.

- **Are your bartenders or servers over-pouring drinks?** Implement portion-control pourers on your liquor bottles. Your pricing is based on a "per shot" basis. If your bartender or waitress is providing a "shot and a half" in every drink, they're in effect giving away one in every three bottles of liquor, for free.

- **Are your employees failing to charge for add-on items,** such as coffee, tea and extra sauces? If you notice that a certain employee never seems to serve customers that drink of coffee, or buy an add-on item that other servers' customers buy, investigate further and take appropriate action if you find any deception taking place.

- **Mistakes?** Have your employees place any "mistakes" on a shelf for management review and notate as to why and how the mistake occurred. Using (and sticking to) this method will make certain that employees and managers take spoilage and waste seriously, as well as deter theft.

- **Do you monitor employee meals?** All employee meals should be paid for at the time of ordering, unless you offer them for free, in which case they should be signed for and noted by a manager.

- **If you wanted to serve a meal without ringing it up, how easy would it be?** Consider the ability of your servers to get food from the kitchen without recording sales and then give those items to the customers, friends, or worse - the trunk of their car.

Register Practices

Your earnings go through a number of steps before they make it into your checking account. The first of those steps is the journey it makes from the customer to the cash register. It is vital that you have rigorous register procedures in place and that all staff is fully aware of the importance of sticking to the rules. Here are a few essential guidelines:

- **Cashiers should never have access to the keys you use to display and print your end-of-day sales reports.** Any incidence where a cash register is "rung off" should be noted and performed by a manager. A new cash drawer should be used from that point onwards.

- **Monitor all voids and over-rings.** If an employee makes a lot of "mistakes," they may be taking cash out of their drawer after a customer has paid and left the premises. The same goes for under-ringing of checks. Always watch and match your checks to your register rolls.

- **Ensure all guest checks are numbered** and the numbers are kept on file alongside the server's name. If checks don't match the total rung up on the register, you want to have as much hard evidence as possible should you decide to terminate an employee.

- **Any guest check voided because of error still**

needs to be accounted for. This will allow you to spot when any check goes "missing" and make sure that the payment for every check makes it into the register and not into an employee's pocket.

Giveaways

Many establishments give food and drinks away to customers as part of their promotional expenses. A two-for-one deal or a free drink for every main course is a great incentive to get people through the door, but make sure you're not being ripped off in the process. Here's how:

- **Use a separate key.** If you occasionally give customers free drinks or meals, either as complimentary gifts or as part of a promotion, use a separate key on your register to ring up those giveaways and ensure a manager knows about every incidence, either by signing for it or by receiving a voucher. This tightens control on giveaways, maximizes your profits and allows you to maintain incentives.

- **Monitor coupon usage.** Destroy all complimentary meal and discount coupons you receive to ensure that the same vouchers aren't being used twice. Handing a used promotional voucher back to friends is a common ploy used by unreliable employees to defraud your establishment.

- **Employees often enjoy free or reduced meals while they're working.** But, you still need to account for these expenses in order to keep accurate tabs on your inventory and to be able to forecast your purchasing needs.

- **Are your employees consuming too many free drinks at the bar after work?** Many restaurants have a "one free drink" after-work policy, which may become a two- or three-drink policy without you realizing it. Consider implementing a rule whereby only management can dispense the free drink.

Security

Money isn't the only thing you need to worry about being stolen. Inventory and supplies are an internal thief's "bread and butter" - a steak, a few knives and spoons, a bottle of champagne or two. Everything you own needs to be watched and secured whenever possible. Safeguard the following vulnerable areas of your establishment:

- **Always be sure to lock your bar inventory when the bar is not open for service.** This will actively deter employees and wandering customers from engaging in petty theft. It will also allow you to identify exactly when and where any losses occur.

- **Make sure you have locks on all of your storage areas.** Establish rules as to who can get their hands on the keys. Your local locksmith can help you not only with the locks, but also with more sophisticated measures, such as closed circuit cameras and card swipe systems.

- **Lock the office.** Limiting access to your office areas will prevent theft of valuables as well as valuable information.

- **Kitchen layout.** When designing or refitting a

kitchen, locate your freezers and walk-in coolers as far from the back door as possible. Making it harder to sneak out high-cost items can only benefit your fight to avoid loss through theft.

- **Implement a robbery plan for your employees.** If the unthinkable should occur, you want to ensure that both your employees and customers are as safe as possible and that your cash is hard to get. Talk to a security expert and your local law enforcement officials to determine the best plan of action in the event of a robbery.

Correct Cash-Handling Procedures

The correct handling of money is a skill in itself. It should never be left to chance.

- **Leaving the cash register unattended.** Unavoidably, there are often times when employees have to leave their cash register unattended - a situation that almost invites dishonesty. Create a system where either your staff shouldn't have to leave the drawer unattended or they must log on with a pass code to open the drawer. Not only does this prevent theft, but it also allows you to instill confidence in your staff that any errors (or thefts) by someone else won't be attributed to them.

- **Ensure that your cashiers call out the total amount of a transaction.** They should also call out the amount tendered to the customer. This communicates what you are doing with the customer; it also reduces the risk that the customer will claim he or she handed across a larger note than was actually the case. By the same token, make certain your cashier doesn't put any notes into the cash drawer until after the transaction is complete.

- **Train employees to count aloud any change they're handing to the customer.** This ensures that the change is counted three times - once when your cashier takes it out of the drawer, once again when it's being handed to the customer and finally, by the customer while it's being handed to them. This reduces the incidence of costly mistakes, misunderstandings and employee theft.

- **Night drops.** If employees have to make night bank drops, make sure that they're accompanied by another employee.

- **Have all guest checks accounted for before an employee leaves.** Keeping strict control of the money within your business will significantly lower theft opportunities, not to mention man-hours spent trying to figure out shortages.

Reducing Customer Fraud

Your customers can also be a prime source of loss, especially if your employees are less than careful. Here are some common pitfalls:

- **"The letter scam."** The "customer is always right," yes, but use caution. This scam appears every few years. A letter arrives in the mail or over the fax telling you what a great evening they had at your restaurant. "Food, wine, service; everything was great. We can't wait to come back." The zinger: "The only problem was, of course, when the busboy spilled some wine on my jacket, so enclosed is the bill for $30 for the cleaning."

- **Bad checks are a major source of customer theft.** Try to avoid accepting checks unless you know the customer well. If you absolutely must take a check, be sure to check the ID of the person signing it.

- **Credit cards.** When accepting credit cards, always have your employees check the signature on the card against the signature on the receipt. To ensure they do this, have them write "verified" on the receipt afterwards.

- **Short-changed.** Occasionally, a customer will claim to have been given change for a smaller bill than they originally handed over. In this situation, if it's possible to "Z" the register and run a quick cash count to verify the cash drawer contents, then do so. If you're too busy to close a register, get the customer's name and phone number and tell them you will call them as soon as the drawer has been balanced and forward any overage to them at your own cost. Certainly, you don't want to lose a customer if you can help it, but being an easy target for fraud can do even more damage to your bottom line.

- **"Bundle" notes.** At various times throughout the night, under the supervision of the cashier involved, have your manager "bundle" any notes that number twelve or more in the cash drawer into bundles of ten and then move them to the safe, replacing them in the drawer with signed requisition slips. This keeps the end-of-the-night count simple. It also keeps large amounts of cash out of the place where it's most vulnerable.

- **Easy targets.** Do your table settings include expensive (or even inexpensive) centerpieces that customers might like to take home? Are these centerpieces easily slipped into a pocket or handbag? Consider using centerpieces that are large enough to be left on the table.

- **Walkouts.** In order to prevent customer walkouts, after presenting the bill, the server should return to the table promptly for payment, or at the very least keep a constant eye on the customers. Having your cashier located at the only non-alarmed exit door will not prevent customers from leaving without paying, but it will certainly make such a move more risky for them. If your staff is alert and attentive, your customer walkouts should be cut to a minimum.

Keeping Your Own House in Check

It's all well and good to keep an eye on everyone else, but you need to ensure that your own practices are as secure as everyone else's - this means putting office procedures in place that will limit the chance of theft. The following practical procedures can make a big impact on reducing the operating costs of your restaurant:

- **Never make an outgoing check to "cash," and don't accept them either.** With a "cash" check, anyone could deposit the check as his or her own, or worse; the receiver of the check could bank it and claim it never arrived. Your check is always your last chance for a receipt and security of that check is paramount.

- **Keep all unused checks locked in a safe.**

- **Keep tabs on all check number successions.** Take immediate action if checks go missing. You always have the option of stopping payment if need be, but if you don't spot a problem quickly, you may never get that chance.

- **Limit all access to petty cash.** Petty cash is the number-one area of office fraud. If your petty cash isn't under lock and key, you can almost guarantee it'll find its way out the door.

- **The person who signs your company checks should also be the person that mails them.** This ensures that your checks find their way to the company for which they're intended; it also makes certain you don't pay any "fake" invoices.

- **"Double-check."** The manager responsible for writing deposit slips, counting money and marking the deposit entry in your books should always be "seconded" by another person, especially when it's being deposited, to ensure that nothing goes missing between the office and bank.

- **Reconcile all bank statements** as quickly as possible. If bank reconciliations are delayed and there is a major error in the checkbook, you could end up bouncing checks or being told by the bank that any problem cannot be corrected. Do you need help in learning how to reconcile your bank statement? The following links provide ideas and tips in keeping your financials in order: Quick Books at www.quickbooks.com/support/faqs/qbw2001/122131.html or Mumssie Online at hometown.aol.com/mumssie/bankstatement.html.

Electronic Security

In the restaurant industry, electronic security is a necessity. Consider the following essentials:

- **Back-door security.** Have your back door hooked up to a small buzzer so that anytime it's opened, a small noise sounds letting anyone in the kitchen and office know. Using this feature will also keep customers, inspectors and even the competition from sneaking a peek into your kitchen. Also remember that a wide-open door invites bugs, rodents and outside noise into your kitchen.

- **Utilize an employee login system into your POS wherever possible.** Make sure employees know that these numbers are for their own good and that sharing their numbers puts their safety in jeopardy. Systems like this not only let you keep track of who is opening a register, but also which employees are busiest, fastest and make the least number of mistakes.

- **Install alarms on exit doors marked for "emergency use only."** This will keep your clientele and employees from walking out when they're not supposed to be, as well as keeping outsiders from sneaking into your establishment. For more information on door chimes and alarms, take a look at these online alarm retailers: Chime City at www.chimecity.com or Drive Alert at www.drivealert.com.

- **Visible cameras.** Security cameras, or at the very least, fake cameras, posted at exit doors and cash areas will keep your staff on their toes - and your customers from getting sneaky.

Cut down on breakage and spoilage and increase profits.

CHAPTER NINE

BREAKAGE, STORAGE & SPOILAGE

Breakage Prevention

By following a few simple rules, you can greatly reduce losses from breakage and keep your glassware, tableware and equipment supplies from turning over unnecessarily:

- **Hot pads.** Always have your employees use hot pads when serving meals, thereby reducing breakage incidents when a plate is "too warm."
- **Cooling time.** Ensure that all employees using dishwashing machines give your glassware and tableware ample time to cool before they start moving them around the kitchen. When glassware or ceramics are heated, they have a far lower breakage point and are much more likely to develop small cracks, or worse; break.
- **Correct usage.** Make it clear to your kitchen staff that ceramic bowls are not to be used for things like whisking of eggs or stirring of contents. Such actions will damage your tableware and dramatically lessen their usable lifespan. Provide Tupperware or metalware for these sorts of activities.
- **Silverware.** Have employees dry all silverware before putting it away for an extended period. This

simple activity will ensure that every piece of cutlery is actually clean and will also cut down on rust over a long period.

- **General glassware.** Make sure that all glassware properly fits your glass racks, especially in the dishwasher. If they don't have a snug fit, glasses will do a lot of bouncing around during the wash cycle and while being transported. This will bring their "failure date" a long way forward.

- **Stemmed glassware.** Stemmed glasses are far more susceptible to breakage than most other types of glasses, not to mention generally more expensive. All staff should take extra care in the handling of these items, perhaps even to the point of washing them only by hand.

- **Are your dishes and bowls easy to handle?** Quite often what looks great on a table can be hard for an employee to handle, leading to breakages. Similarly, if your plates aren't easily stackable and thick enough to take the wear and tear of daily restaurant life, you could be wasting money. When choosing dinnerware for your restaurant, take more than just looks into account.

- **Never allow your bar staff to use glasses as ice scoops.** Obvious as this is, we often see this happen. A tiny chip of glass falling into the ice bin can cause a great deal of injury. Bar glassware certainly isn't designed to shovel rocks of ice. Along the same lines, any time a glass breaks in or near an ice bin, the entire ice bin needs to be emptied and the contents disposed of before it can be used in the preparation of another drink. Always line the bin with a plastic bag to make emptying it easier. Use a Saf-T-Ice Scoop Caddie to keep the ice scoop safe from bacteria, dirt and ice burial, available from www.atlantic-pub.com, 800-541-1336, Item # ST-2000, $23.95.

- **Staff should never touch the upper half of a glass in the act of serving a drink.** It's unhygienic and it looks terrible to the customer. Also, the glass will be much more susceptible to breakage if it's being regularly handled in this manner.

- **All glasses and plates need to be inspected,** if only briefly, before they're used to fill an order. A lipstick smudge, chip, crack or remnants of a previous meal or drink are not only off-putting to a customer, but also hazardous to the customer's health.

- **Limit the number of dishes stacked on the warming table,** by the dishwasher and in storage areas. Placing large stacks of dishes on top of each other causes great stress on those at the bottom of the pile. It will also result in your tableware breaking far sooner than it should. Try to avoid piling them any more than a dozen high.

- **Avoid unnecessary handling and transportation of dishes and glassware.** If the journey your dishware takes from the dishwasher to the warmer to the counter to the table is a long one, think about ways to eliminate steps from the process. Is the warmer next to the washer? Does your staff stack loaded dishracks when they're just out of the washer, adding another step to the process? Use your space to your advantage.

Spoiled food is money thrown out the window. Here's how to reduce spoilage to the bare minimum:

- **List all spoiled food on a form.** This allows you to make inventory adjustments, noting whether you're ordering too much of an item, or have an equipment problem; for example, an ineffective cooler.

- **Color code, label and date all food.** Using older food before newer food will ensure you keep losses to a minimum and can see any problems coming in advance. You can also use date stickers so employees know how long an item has been stored. Use dissolvable labels so that the label and adhesive dissolve in any water temperature! Daymark Food Safety Systems manufactures a line of biodegradable labels that will dissolve in under 30 seconds leaving no sticky residue. These labels will adhere to hard plastics and stainless steel containers. Labels are FDA approved for indirect food contact. These food rotation labels may be purchased at www.dissolveaway.com, 800-847-0101.

- **Are your coolers too cold?** Freezing, frost and freezer burn is a major source of spoilage in the kitchen. Make regular inspections of your cooler's temperature. Keep a written chart of when the last checks were performed. Use specialty thermometers for these areas. See www.atlantic-pub.com. Look for fluctuations, or "cold points" in the cooler that differ in temperature from the rest of the area.

- **Different qualities and brands of food may spoil at different rates.** If you happen to change your brand or supplier on a particular line of food, make sure to keep a closer eye on the condition of your stock, taking note of any changes in freshness so that you can alter your purchasing to suit.

- **Eggs at room temperature.** To keep the yokes of your eggs from breaking easily, have any eggs to be used in the coming hours set at room temperature before they're used. This simple piece of advice will keep your eggs in perfect "cracking" condition and keep your wastage to a minimum.

- **Don't refreeze foods.** This will take away from the taste of the food. Sometimes you may have no choice, but if you can keep food in a cooler at a refrigerated temperature and reuse it quickly, you'll be far better off.

- **Spices, sauces and marinades can be pre-prepared** and stored for long periods without spoiling if kept at the right temperature. If a sauce or marinade requires an item with a high spoilage rate, make a large batch and freeze it in small containers to be used as needed, saving on time and money. It also ensures that every meal has a consistent taste.

- **Backup generator.** If your electricity supply went down for half a day, what would happen to your inventory? Save yourself the heartache of watching your food go to waste in the event of a utility problem by purchasing a backup generator. A small generator powerful enough to keep your walk-in cooler up and running at all times, could save you thousands of dollars in lost assets if the unthinkable happens.

- **Monitor your walk-ins and freezers.** Your alarm monitoring company may have a program to monitor the temperature in your freezers and coolers. Or, you could hire a company such as Food Watch, www.foodwatch.com/foodwatch.htm. Their systems accurately and remotely measure the refrigeration efficiency of walk-ins, stand-alone refrigerators or food cases. The patent-pending Compressor Watch sensor attaches to the outside of the compressor motor. The system can also record the amount of time the walk-in door is left open. The system is operated via a telephone line.

- **Electrical failure.** If the power fails to resume within 1-2 days, or if a mechanical problem hasn't been fixed, keep the freezer closed. Use dry ice to keep the freezer temperatures below freezing and to prevent spoilage. Locating where dry ice can be purchased now will save valuable time later. Consider calling other restaurants, your vendors, or cold-storage companies, should the problem involve further delays. Plan ahead now.

Storage

A well-organized storage system and clearly defined procedures can significantly reduce your restaurant's operating costs. Consider the following possibilities:

- **Correct stacking.** The improper stacking of storage containers can result in spills, breakage and worse; accidents. Ensure that if you use storage containers, they stack properly and are easy to handle. Stacking items on top of one another in your cooler might seem to be the most productive way to utilize your limited space, but such a system makes cleaning and access to certain items very difficult.

- **Shelving.** A good shelving system that is flexible enough to allow you to change shelf heights is essential. It makes the most of the available space, allows easy access to every item in your fridge and makes cleaning a breeze.

- **Reuse containers.** When you receive deliveries like flour, sugar and salt in large five-gallon buckets, you might be able to reuse them for storing dry materials. Buckets like these are usually airtight and designed for maximum protection of the contents. So, rather than tossing them, clean them, re-label them and utilize them. Do not, however, use them for ice storage.

- **Use a designated ice transport container** such as Saf-T-Ice Tote. Ice transfer is a cross-contamination disaster waiting to happen in most food service operations. Saf-T-Ice Totes help you control this serious food safety danger! The units are made of tough, transparent, durable polycarbonate. The 6-gallon size keeps the carrying weight at safe levels. Features include a stainless steel bail handle for easy carrying/emptying. Saf-T-Ice Totes are dishwasher safe, meet health department requirements for dedicated food service containers and are available from www.atlantic-pub.com, 800-541-1336, Item #SI-6000, $79.95 for a pack of two.

- **Canned vs. fresh.** Don't automatically use fresh fruit and vegetables if canned alternatives can be used without cutting back on meal quality. Canned tomatoes, artichoke hearts, chili peppers, pears, etc., can all be used in many meals without a big loss in flavor. The trade off is easier storage and a big drop in price and spoilage rates.

- **Rotate stock when receiving deliveries.** There's no better time to perform a stock rotation than when you're first putting away fresh items. Failure to do so can make it harder to differentiate what's new and what's old.

Hygiene

In financial terms, poor hygiene can seriously damage your operation. Even a single incidence can ruin your good reputation and force you out of business. Insist on the following preventative measures:

- **Kitchen staff should always wear hats and gloves** and keep hair tied back when working with food. Failure to use preventative measures such as these can see you losing big money when an expensive meal is returned because of a single hair being where it shouldn't.

- **Storing leftovers.** When storing leftovers, make certain to wrap items tightly in Saran wrap, or in airtight Tupperware. For example, keeping cut lettuce, tomatoes and onions in airtight containers will go a long way towards preventing them from turning brown and limp. If food is stored using non-airtight methods, it will dry out and quickly become unusable. Also, exposed food invites germs, bugs and spills.

- **Storing hot food.** When putting away hot food, such as soups and stews, divide the batch into smaller batches and allow to cool in shallow pans. Alternatively, place the pans in a shallow ice bath. This will help cool the food quickly and avoid the possibility of contamination. Consider a blast chiller unit or small, easy-to-use plastic "Flash

Chill" containers designed to reduce the core temperature of the content; available at www.atlantic-pub.com.

Rodent and Bug Prevention

One mouse; that's all it takes to send your customers running. No matter how clean you think your kitchen is, it only takes one bug to classify it as a failure in the eyes of your patrons. Take measures to prevent the unthinkable:

- **Receipt procedures.** Bugs and rodents can come into your kitchen in many ways, particularly under doors, through cracks in the walls and most often, inside deliveries of fruit and vegetables. Ensure that each and every delivery of produce is checked outside the kitchen, if possible, so that any insects or rodents aren't brought into your food prep area.

- **You don't always need to spend a lot on an exterminator** for your premises. For information on do-it-yourself pest control, try the following Web sites: Do Your Own Pest Control at www.do-yourownpestcontrol.com or Pest Control Supplies at www.pest-control-supplies.com.

- **Bug-free kitchen.** The only way to ensure bugs and rodents don't enter your kitchen is to make it clean enough to starve them out. This means no food left on floors and surfaces and regular pest-control visits. The use of roach traps is another good hidden, preventative measure.

- **Don't ever store dry foods in boxes or out in the open.** Rather, use sealable clear plastic storage containers to prevent mice, worms, cockroaches and ants from finding their way in. Cambro manufacturing, www.cambro.com, makes a complete line of these products for food service use.

INDEX